Watchmen
ON
THE
Walls

Watchmen ON THE Walls

An Eyewitness Account of Israel's Fight for Independence
from the Journal of

Hannah Hurnard

BROADMAN
& HOLMAN
PUBLISHERS

Nashville, Tennessee

This edition issued by special arrangement with
Monarch Publications Ltd.,
Broadway House, The Broadway, Crowborough,
East Sussex, TN6 1HQ, England

ISBN 0–8054–1399–5

Published in 1998 by Broadman & Holman Publishers,
Nashville, Tennessee
Acquisitions and Development Editor: Leonard Goss
Page Design: Anderson Thomas Design
Typesetting: TF Designs, Mt. Juliet, Tennessee

Library of Congress Cataloging-in-Publication Data

Hurnard, Hannah.
Watchmen on the walls / Hannah Hurnard.
    p.   cm.
ISBN 0–8054–1399–5
1. Hurnard, Hannah.   2. Jerusalem—History—Siege, 1948—Bibliography.   3. Israel-Arab War, 1948-1949—Personal narratives. British.
4. Missionaries—Jerusalem—Biography.   5. Church's Ministry Among
Jewish People—Bibliography.   I. Title.
DS126.94.J4H87   1998
956.04'2–dc21

                                                    97–42544
                                                    CIP

1 2 3 4 5 02 01 00 99 98

Dedicated with warm appreciation to
Rev. and Mrs. Ronald and Laura Adeney,
and to Mrs. Ursula Jones,
for each of whom the memories recorded here
are poignant and personal.

Contents

Foreword
by John Wood

Setting the Scene

One early reviewer said of *Watchmen on the Walls* that "here we have a slice of history, a little autobiography, some lessons on the life of prayer, a thriller, and, finally, a piece of Biblical interpretation." In August 1950 it was reported that many secular Jews in Israel were reading *Watchmen*. Even now, half a century after the events it describes, Hannah Hurnard's vivid journal perfectly recaptures the sights and sounds of those turbulent times. Yet from start to finish, it breathes a spirit of quite extraordinary composure amid all the chaos and carnage of a city at war.

The Writer

By any reckoning, Hannah Hurnard was a most unlikely war heroine. Not only was she from a Quaker family with pacifist principles, she had been an introspective timid girl with a fearful stammer, who hated being with other people but was terrified to be shut up in a room on her own.

In the event, it was a life-changing encounter with Christ at Keswick in Cumbria, during the Christian Convention there in July 1924, that triggered the transformation in her life. It resulted in her becoming first a student at Ridgelands Bible College in Wimbledon, southwest London, and subsequently a worker for four years with the Friends' Evangelistic Band, now the Fellowship for Evangelizing Britain's Villages (FEBV).

Then, after a visit to the Middle East with her father and brother in early 1929, partly to give aid to Armenian refugees but also to visit the new Jewish settlements in Palestine, Hannah Hurnard sailed for Haifa three years later as a temporary helper with the British Jews Society. As it happened, her "temporary" sojourn in the Holy Land lasted for the better part of fifty years.

At first, Hannah found it difficult to discover her proper role at Haifa. However, she set about adjusting to a new culture and learning the local language(s). In addition to taking little services in the waiting room of Dr. Churcher's clinic, she also taught English to groups of very lively Jewish children four days a week.

But as time went by, her specific calling became abundantly clear. She had a flair for establishing a rapport with everyone she met. The German she had started to learn at finishing school in Horgen, Switzerland, in 1923–1924 enabled her to relate to the colonists she met in German-speaking kibbutzim across the north of the country.

Eventually, her skill in both Hebrew and Arabic also began to develop.

The metamorphosis was really quite extraordinary. From being a morbid, self-centered teenager with a crippling stammer, Hannah developed into a lively, outgoing personality with the gift of communication. Not only did she pioneer a face-to-face, one-to-one, two-by-two evangelistic work, first among Jewish settlers, then in all the Arab towns and villages throughout the country; she also demonstrated considerable leadership qualities as well, enlisting the help of numerous expatriate workers from several different societies in the land and organizing their visitation in a systematic way.

Her courage rose with danger. It is true that in many kibbutzim and Arab villages, people warmed to her. But there was also hostility. Her books and Bibles would be torn or burned. Orthodox Jews would sometimes spit in the dust and curse the name she loved. In many Arab villages, she braved dark-eyed, dagger-wielding, stone-throwing activists, out to avenge themselves on their British overlords.

But this rather aristocratic young lady, from a country whose government was hated by ardent Zionists and Arab nationalists alike, remained undaunted. The little Austin car her father had donated for village work was a familiar sight as it bumped along unmade tracks to out-of-the-way settlements or nosed along roads notorious for sniper fire and land mines. When the car eventually expired from old age, overuse, and Hannah Hurnard's somewhat erratic driving style, it was replaced by the blue Morris 8 van with closed-in sides, which features so prominently in *Watchmen*.

An Unlikely Appointment

At first, Hannah Hurnard had worked with the Free Church Society, BJS, which became part of what is now Christian Witness to Israel (CWI). But as her village work developed, so did her contacts with colleagues from several other societies. Like so many Christians influenced by the Keswick movement, Hannah was most at home in an inter-denominational environment.

So it was not at all surprising that when CMJ's (The Church's Ministry Among Jewish People) hospital in Jerusalem needed a new housekeeper in 1947, Hannah's name was high on the list of possible replacements, especially as her older sister, Ruth, a qualified doctor, had married the editor of CMJ's publications, Rev. William N. Carter.

By this time, Hannah Hurnard had been evacuated from Jerusalem, along with all other ex-patriates who stood in danger of being targeted and taken hostage by Jewish fighters determined to end Britain's mandate, and was back home in Lexden, Colchester, after an absence of eight years. Together with former colleagues also exiled from the land of their adoption, Hannah prayed for the ongoing work in what was then known as "Palestine," especially when CMJ wrote to say that a new housekeeper was needed at the hospital in Jerusalem. It never occurred to her that she might be the answer to her own prayers!

It has to be said that Hannah's housekeeping skills were negligible. Even her father, the austere Samuel Fennell Hurnard, felt she would have been better employed working as a village evangelist in Syria until such time as the situation in Palestine improved. He knew as well as anyone that while she was superb as a village worker she was a non-starter when it came to keeping house! So the follow-up letter from CMJ inviting her to the post caused him considerable consternation but simply convulsed dear Hannah with unrestrained merriment!

However, it had to be taken seriously. At last she came to realize that her excellent relationships with both Jews and Arabs, plus her facility in English, Hebrew, German, and Arabic, meant that she was well placed to reach across the racial and cultural divides among the hospital patients in Jerusalem. Moreover, her long experience of facing both Jewish and Arab hostility in the land enabled her to encourage doctors, nurses, and auxiliary staff who were under siege in the midst of war-torn Jerusalem.

So, because the former housekeeper had trained her staff so well, Hannah accepted the position as her successor on the understanding that everyone realize she was most certainly not the ideal choice so far as the practicalities of running a hospital were concerned!

It so happened that the first speaker at the missionary meeting she had attended on the Saturday morning of the convention that changed her life in 1924 had been Dr. H. J. Orr-Ewing of Jerusalem, who had spoken about the problems of treating patients in a hospital where up to fourteen different languages were being spoken at any one time! Now here she was, twenty-three years later, driving up the mountain road to Jerusalem in October 1947, ready to serve as housekeeper in that very same hospital.

On the Street of the Prophets

CMJ was one of the first, if not *the* first Christian society to develop a medical ministry on what was then described as "the mission field." Opened on April 13, 1897, the new hospital, which replaced an earlier one, served the poor and aging Jewish population of the city with outstanding success, so much so that Jewish benefactors in Britain

combined with others to establish specifically Jewish insti-
tutions to care for their hitherto neglected compatriots.

But CMJ's hospital was never short of patients, even
after Jewish clinics had been set up and local religious leaders had warned their people against using the services of
"Christian" doctors. In 1909, Dr. Percy D'Erf Wheeler
bemoaned the fact that he was having to turn away many
needy cases because there were not enough beds. Yet he
treated a total of 493 patients on the three wards of his hospital in one period of twelve weeks.

The hospital buildings, which presently house the Anglican International School, face to the Street of the Prophets
in Jewish West Jerusalem. However, Christ Church,
CMJ's worship center and guest house, a mile away, is situated opposite the citadel inside the Old City, which by
1948 was predominantly Arab.

Christ Church had been founded in 1840 during the episcopate of the first Anglican Bishop in Jerusalem, Rt. Rev.
Michael Solomon Alexander. As the son of an English rabbi
from Posen, Alexander himself had become a rabbi in Nor-
wich and a Shochet in Plymouth, after first spending time in
Hannah's hometown of Colchester. Indeed it was while acting as a private tutor to Jewish children there, at the behest
of the chief rabbi, that he had first encountered the London
Society for Promoting Christianity Among the Jews (now
known as "CMJ," The Church's Ministry Among Jewish
People), and had begun his search for a personal Messiah.

Now, more than a century after his episcopate in Jerusalem, Hannah Hurnard found herself commuting between
CMJ's two main centers in the city, which were under
threat from both of the warring factions.

The End of the Mandate

Back in November 1917, the Balfour Declaration had promised the Jews a homeland in Palestine, provided the rights of the indigenous population were not infringed upon. But no one had quite worked out how the hopes and aspirations of both peoples could be justly accommodated in such a circumstance. In the course of time, Britain made promises to both Arabs and Jews that proved to be incompatible and, in trying to please all parties, succeeded only in pleasing none.

The longer Britain's mandate continued, the more impossible it became. As more and more Jewish refugees arrived, Arab leaders incited riots against the British. But when the number of Jewish immigrants was severely cut back to allay Arab fears, Jewish leaders were outraged that so many of their compatriots were refused entry into Palestine.

In January 1947, Hannah was one of many British women and children airlifted to Egypt in "Operation Polly," fondly renamed "Operation Folly"! On March 2, martial law was imposed after twenty British soldiers and civilians were killed. In April, barracks near Tel Aviv were blown up. Also two Hebrew Christians were kidnapped but later released unharmed. On May 4, Jewish activists broke into the jail at Acre (Akko) and liberated 251 prisoners, including Arabs as well as Jews. Then in July, after British naval ratings had boarded the *Exodus* in Haifa Harbor, its five thousand Jewish passengers were refused entry to their promised homeland and found themselves being summarily sent to a refugee camp in Cyprus.

By September, the Labor Government in London decided to relinquish the Mandate. It had become unworkable. Then after a further bomb outrage in Tel Aviv in which nine British personnel were killed, the United Nations

decided on November 29 to partition Palestine, with Jerusalem being designated as an international city.

Thus the scene was set for the crucial showdown between
jubilant Jews and noncompliant Arabs. As one of only three
CMJ expatriates allowed to go on living in Jerusalem, Hannah Hurnard found herself caught up in the conflict whenever she commuted between the hospital and Christ Church
or ferried friends to the airport.

A Triple Cord

Here and there in this journal, we catch tantalizing
glimpses of Hannah Hurnard's two companions. And like
Oliver Twist, we keep asking for more. Each deserves more
than a passing mention.

Miss Ruth Clark, one of three sisters who served with
CMJ, had first come to Jerusalem in 1909 as a teacher at
the girls' school, which was housed in what is now part of
the Christ Church guest house. Later she became headmistress, keeping the school open during the Arab strikes in
1926, even when bombs exploded in the vicinity. On
March 7, 1948, there were over one hundred pupils, of
whom more than seventy were Jewish.

Ruth made no secret of her aims. "In our school," she
once said, "Jew and Arab grow to love each other as they
learn and pray together, and as they come to realize their
common need of God's help and guidance day by day."
When a notable Jewish activist was killed by British security forces, Ruth visited the homes of every pupil affected by
the tragedy.

Now, in 1948, Ruth was once again compelled to face
upheaval and danger. In early February, eighteen panes of
glass at the hospital were shattered when the offices of the
British newspaper *Palestine Post*, half a mile away, were

bombed. Then on February 22, sirens wailed as ambulances ferried the injured to the hospital following a bomb outrage in the famous Ben Yehuda Street. Sadly, some died.

Inevitably, anti-British feeling escalated still further, and most British workers left for home. It is typical of Ruth Clark, that with the eventual removal of the Jewish section of her school to the grounds of CMJ's hospital in West Jerusalem, she continued caring for the children in her charge, while Miss Abramson cared for the Arab and Armenian pupils at Christ Church. In 1963, Ruth was honored with the MBE in the Queen's New Year's Honors List.

Ronald Adeney, a lively quick-minded young clergyman from a notable Anglican family, several of whom have served in the ranks of CMJ, was a relative newcomer to the country when hostilities broke out, having arrived in time to help with the Easter services at Christ Church in 1947. But he possessed a vigorous faith and a winsome personality; and throughout the turmoil in Jerusalem that fateful year, he demonstrated quite extraordinary maturity of judgment and character.

It is not hard to imagine the three intrepid workers, gathering around the harmonium in the hospital chapel of an evening, or between lulls in the fighting, singing well-loved Sankey and Keswick hymns, with Hannah at the keyboard. "A cord of three strands is not quickly broken," the preacher rightly said (Eccles. 4:12), and all three of them emerged from the conflict strengthened in faith and fitted for notable service in the days ahead.

For Rev. Ronald Adeney and his wife, the future brought the fulfillment of pioneering CMJ's new Stella Carmel Conference Center, in the Druze village of Isfiya, some ten kilometers from Haifa along the Carmel ridge. There he and Laura established a work that still flourishes as a guest house for tourists, a worship center for the growing Messianic congregation in the locality, and a place where both Arab and Jewish believers can meet. Later, Adeney became director of CMJ's work throughout Israel.

For Hannah, the future included life as a world traveler; enlisting Intercessors for Israel in Central America, Switzerland, UK, and Australasia; and becoming the celebrated writer of several best-sellers, starting with *Watchmen on the Walls*, which was first published by CMJ in 1950.

John Wood
Formerly CMJ's Regional Adviser
for East Anglia Colchester 1997

Introduction

The events of this book cover a period of twelve months, during which time one of the most momentous events in the history of the Jewish people—the birth of the New Jewish State of Israel—took place. This period falls into two parts: (1) from November 29, 1947, when the United Nations' Council voted for the partition of Palestine into Arab and Jewish states, until May 14, 1948, with the ending of the British Mandate in Palestine; and (2) from May 15, 1948, when the new State of Israel was proclaimed, through the Siege of Jerusalem, till December 3, 1948, when the Sincere Truce came into force in Jerusalem.

This is a personal record kept by one of twelve Protestant missionaries who remained in the Jewish area of besieged Jerusalem. It is sent forth as an account of the wonderful mercy and goodness of God during these historic twelve months, but even more particularly, as a trumpet call for prayer and intercession to the people of God from the little group of Christ's "watchmen on the walls of Jerusalem."

"I have set watchmen upon thy walls, O Jerusalem, which shall never hold their peace day nor night: ye that make mention of the LORD, keep not silence, and give him no rest, till he establish, and till he make Jerusalem a praise in the earth" (Isa. 62:6–7).

ISRAEL

ARMISTICE LINE ....

LEBANON

SYRIA

● ACRE

TIBERIAS

HAIFA ●

NAZARETH

● BEISAN

TULKARM ●

● NABLUS

JAFFA
TEL AVIV ●

RAMALLAH ●

REHOVOT ●

● JERICHO

JERUSALEM ●

BETHLEHEM ●

● GAZA

HEBRON ●

BEERSHEBA

I S R A E L

J O R D A N

NEGEV

E G Y P T

● AQABA

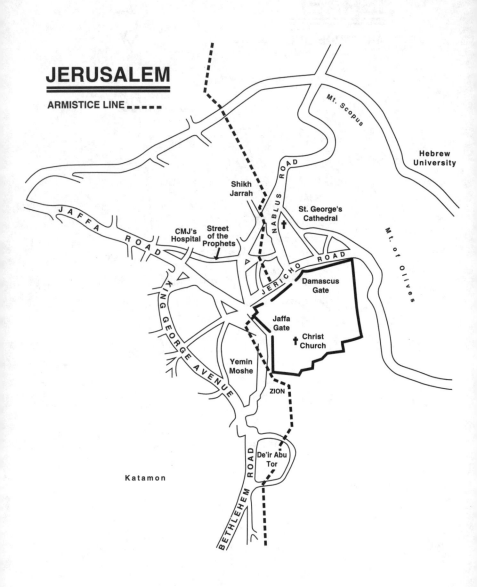

JERUSALEM

ARMISTICE LINE ▪ ▪ ▪ ▪ ▪

Mt. Scopus

Hebrew
University

Shikh
Jarrah

St. George's
Cathedral

Mt. of Olives

CMJ's
Hospital

Street
of the
Prophets

NABLUS ROAD

JERICHO ROAD

Damascus
Gate

JAFFA ROAD

Jaffa
Gate

Christ
Church

KING GEORGE AVENUE

Yemin
Moshe

ZION

De'ir Abu
Tor

Katamon

BETHLEHEM ROAD

Part 1

The End
of a Chapter

1 *A City Divided Against Itself*

*A*dvent Sunday, November 30, 1947, was a memorable day in the history of Jerusalem. We were wakened in the middle of the night by sounds of revelry. The whole of the Jewish quarter of Jerusalem seemed to have turned out into the streets at 1:30 A.M. shouting and cheering and letting off firecrackers while cars, broadcasting from loudspeakers, toured the streets. The commotion increased until dawn, making further sleep almost impossible. At midnight the radio had announced that the United Nations had decided, by thirty-three votes to thirteen, to adopt the plan of partitioning Palestine. As a result the Jewish people had gone nearly wild with joy.

With the coming of daylight, the streets became more and more packed. The population seemed intoxicated with excitement and happiness. It was quite impossible to drive down to Christ Church, just inside the Jaffa Gate, for morning service, as every inch of road and pavement was packed with rejoicing multitudes. Two of us decided to try to walk to the church, but once outside the gate of the English Mission Hospital, we could hardly move, so tightly were the crowds wedged together.

What a scene it was! Every car and bus was packed inside and out with rejoicing revelers. They sat, three or four astride the hoods of the cars and four or five on the roofs, so that the overladen vehicles could only crawl forward inch by inch, or, unable to move at all, remained stationary in the middle of the road, thus adding to the congestion and confusion. The few policemen on point duty evidently realized their impotence among these seething masses and, though refusing to desert the traffic islands, gave up all attempts at control and concentrated on clinging, almost literally, to their posts, buffeted and surrounded by a sea of rejoicing humanity, while the overweighed traffic piled up in the jammed streets. None of the officials seemed to have realized the delirious joy the Proclamation of Partition was to evoke in the hearts of the Jewish people, and so they were unprepared to cope with the situation.

As we wriggled and poked and pushed our way through the surging mass around us, listening to the exultant cheering and shouts in Hebrew of "Israel lives! Long live Israel!" I remembered that it was Advent Sunday, and the thought flashed into my mind, *What if this rejoicing city had turned out in this way to greet their long-awaited King and Messiah? How marvelous if all this joy and exultation was being outpoured in welcome of him. One day it would be so. Was not this very scene of rejoicing a sign and promise that his advent must be near? First a restored Israel, and then the coming of their King.*

At last we struggled through the crowds and out into the Arab quarter. What a contrast we found there. Closed shops, almost empty streets, a silence ominous after the revelry in the Jewish area. Little groups of Arab men were collected here and there, talking over the hateful news and listening sullenly to the riotous noise and shouts of "Israel shall live!" that came echoing down from distant streets. One section of the city was rejoicing and exulting; the other was seething with bitterness.

It was another great contrast to pass into the quiet and peace of the church and to sing the Advent hymns and bow in glad worship before the One who once, in great humility and riding on an ass, had entered this ancient city while rejoicing multitudes thronged around him and hailed him as Messiah so soon before they crucified him. The blind girls from the school in Beit Jala sang to us in their lovely and touching voices, "Jesus is coming again." Here was joy and hope of quite another kind. When he comes again, Israel shall live indeed and become a blessing to the whole world.

All day long the shouting and the excitement continued, until complete exhaustion at last overcame the revelers and the streets gradually emptied. The day of rejoicing was over, and the months of strife and agonizing effort had begun. The very next day, December 1, there were Arab counter-demonstrations, as a result of which seven Jews were killed, and a three-day Arab strike was announced. That evening I was invited to supper at Bishop Gobat School, just outside the Old City wall, but a telephone message came to say that buses and cars from the Jewish area were being stoned and attacked at the Jaffa Gate, and it was quite unsafe to drive down there. A chasm, which was to divide the Old and the

New City, had opened in the course of a few hours, and Jerusalem has been two cities, not one, ever since.[1]

Looking back now, it is extraordinary to see how, in the course of one day and night, the whole situation in Palestine changed. From that time on, life took on a totally new aspect. Had a real gulf opened between the past and the present, the change could not have been more complete. In one day, the long years of increasing tension between the Jews and Arabs seemed to crystallize into a clear-cut cleavage. What many politicians had decided was an impossibility had happened. Partition became an actual fact, though not in the form anyone had foreseen, nor with the precise boundaries decided upon by the United Nations. But partition actually began that day, and in the course of a few weeks it had become so obvious a phenomenon that nobody could deny its existence, though not wanting to acknowledge it.

A three-day Arab strike was immediately proclaimed. All Arab shops and places of business were closed, while the men gathered in the mosques, listening to inflammatory speeches.

The strike had an immediate effect upon our mission hospital, for although it was situated in Jewish Jerusalem, it had been opened when Palestine was still under the Turks and the Jewish population was comparatively small. All the domestic staff, both men and women, were Arabs, and ever since its beginning the hospital had dealt mainly with Arab tradesmen. Every day one of the menservants took the hospital donkey to the Arab market in the Old City and bought fruit, vegetables, and groceries. Arab women coming in from the villages supplied us with hundreds of eggs each week and also with our daily supply of milk. There had been many other strikes in past years, but always these village women had continued to bring their goods to the hospital, even if the market itself was closed.

But on the day the strike started, two days after partition was voted for, the daily supply of produce to the hospital ceased, never to start again. I was temporarily acting as hospital housekeeper and came down that first morning to find that no bread, milk, eggs, fruit, or vegetables had arrived or would arrive. There was, of course, enough tinned food to meet our needs for a few days, but the milk and bread situation was urgent. The Arab market was closed, so it was no use going there, and as a great deal of the fruit and vegetables sold in Jewish shops came from neighboring Arab villages, such shops had at once been besieged by Jewish buyers and quickly emptied of their supplies. I therefore decided to take Assad, our Arab servant, in our van and drive out to Ain Karim, the village from which the women brought our daily milk. It is the traditional birthplace of John the Baptist and lies about five miles west of Jerusalem.

As soon as we left the city and began to wind down the mountainside, we found that rows of stone barricades had been built right across the steep, narrow road, and gangs of men and boys, armed with stones, rocks, and clubs had assembled on the slopes, ready to attack all comers. We nearly suffered a nasty stoning, but fortunately we saw the first gang while we were still out of their range, and we both got out of the van immediately and went on foot to meet them so that they could see that Assad was an Arab. He tried to persuade them to let him walk to Ain Karim in search of milk for the hospital, but they said it was impossible and assured us we were lucky to be allowed to turn around and leave unharmed.

It was no easy matter turning the car on that narrow mountain road, with cliffs rising on one side and a steep precipice on the other. I was indeed thankful to be allowed to perform this maneuver without undergoing a bombardment with stones and clubs. The whole atmosphere was charged with violent excitement, and other gangs were already hurrying up the hill to share in the attack. So we retreated.

We then drove to our Jewish baker and found that the nonarrival of the hospital bread was due to one of their delivery vans having been burned by Jewish attackers. I was able to take our supply of bread to the hospital, as well as some tins of milk. But from that day on, all the roads into Jerusalem were subject to attack, and supplies for the Jewish area had to be brought in by convoys protected by British troops. Fruits and vegetables almost disappeared from the shops; later on, completely so, and meat supplies ceased from the very beginning. For the nine months from December till the following September, only one ration of meat was distributed to Jewish civilians.

It became plain at once that, as soon as the Arab strike was over, we would have to fetch all our supplies from the Arab market, and not make ourselves a burden on Jewish shops even if they had been able to supply everything we needed. So tense and bitter was the feeling between the two peoples that it was unsafe for our Arab servant to pass through the Jewish area with his donkey. I was therefore obliged to drive him to the market every day and fetch him home again with a vanload of stores. The poor man would sit cowering on the floor at the back of the van, denuded of his Arab headdress, trembling with apprehension lest the van should be stopped and searched and he would be dragged out and beaten or kicked to death. For as each day passed, and Arab attacks on the Jewish population intensified, it naturally happened that Jewish feeling became more and more enraged.

After a few weeks it was obvious to us that all of our Arab menservants would have to leave the hospital, for it was not safe for them to remain in the Jewish area. Their homes were in a neighboring village, and for a time we kept them safe in the compound and never asked them to venture outside the gate, unless I took them in the van. But by the end of December the situation had become so dangerous that they gave notice in a body, and we had to carry on as best we could without any men helpers. We were indeed thankful that all the maids remained gallantly at their posts, even though it became difficult for them, too, to venture outside the compound except in the van.

On the very first evening of the Arab strike, a number of Jewish shops near Barclay's Bank were burned to the ground. And as the days passed, the Arabs burned and blew up more and more Jewish shops on the border areas and in the main commercial center, where Jewish and Arab shops stood side by side. For weeks it was a daily occurrence to hear loud explosions, which meant that more shops in the commercial center had been destroyed. All the Jewish population in that quarter had withdrawn into the wholly Jewish area, leaving their shops and homes to be rifled and ransacked. And naturally it became necessary for Arabs living in the Jewish area to leave their shops and their homes and to move into the Old City.

On December 4 the British authorities placed the whole Arab quarter under a two-day curfew to prevent further violence. When this curfew was lifted, the Jewish and Arab areas were already distinct and separate entities. No cars or buses could pass from one area to the other, and all intercourse ceased, except for those who were granted special permits. I was among this number and was allowed to pass into the Arab area day by day in order to fetch supplies for the hospital.

The whole mission work, especially the medical and educational, was now situated in Jewish Jerusalem, but Christ Church and the girls' school were in the Old City, just inside the Jaffa Gate. By December 8, only a week later, it had become impossible for the hundred Jewish day girls to reach the school. It was decided therefore to divide the school in two. The Arab and the Christian girls were to continue at the main school, and the Jewish girls and teachers were to move temporarily into two empty wards in the mission hospital.

By this time the number of patients attending the hospital was rapidly decreasing as it became increasingly difficult to move about. Arabs of course could no longer come, and many of our patients lived in the Jewish quarter of the Old City, which was now completely isolated from the rest of Jewish Jerusalem. The authorities wished to evacuate these Jews, but they refused to move, and until the end of the mandate, supplies were taken to them by military convoys. When the mandate ended and there was no foreign power to intervene, the Jewish quarter of the Old City was obliged to surrender to the Arab Legion.

On December 10 we heard that a Jewish convoy that had ventured out without a military escort to carry food to a group of lone Jewish settlements in the Hebron area had been ambushed, and nine men in the convoy had been killed and their bodies mutilated. I had several times visited these lonely settlements on the mountains, now so tragically isolated in enemy territory, and it was dreadful to picture their situation. How long could they hold out against attack by overwhelming numbers?

Two days later Jewish reprisals started in Jerusalem, and a number of Arab shops were blown up. Driving about in unidentified cars had become so dangerous that we fixed large red crosses on the van to show that it was from the hospital. That evening we heard that one of the BOAC vans on its way to Lydda Airport had been stopped by Arabs and burned; the one or two Jews in it had been killed.

It must not be supposed that the police and military were idle at this time. But an eruption was taking place that was rapidly becoming beyond their power to quell. We had experienced the premonitory quakings and tremblings for years, but now it was in full blast and was to cost the lives of many British men, during the last months before the mandate ended, in the dangerous work of trying to maintain peace and intervening in Arab-Jewish attacks.

Every day that passed brought new scenes of violence. On December 13, just as we left Jaffa Gate with a vanload of supplies, there was a tremendous explosion. Within a few moments, Arab taxis were tearing through the streets, carrying wounded and dead to the government hospital. We were obliged to take refuge, for there was a sharp outbreak of shooting close at hand. We were told that a bomb had been thrown from a taxi at a crowded bus standing at Damascus Gate, right in the Arab area, by Jews wearing Arab dress. Three people were killed outright, and twenty-two were injured. When the streets were a little quieter, we tried to return to our hospital.

By this time, two weeks after partition, there were barriers across all the main roads at the junctions of the Arab and Jewish quarters, manned by British police in order to prevent terrorists on both sides from smuggling in explosives or perpetrating other acts of violence. And now, as soon as we reached our usual barrier, we found the whole road crowded with Jewish people who had heard the explosion and rushed to the barrier to see what was happening.

At the barrier the police, of course, stopped me and asked for my British identity card, and also, as usual, opened the door of the van to make sure that I was not smuggling explosives. They discovered the terrified Assad crouching on the floor and said at once that it was impossible for me to drive him through such a crowd. For though the absence of windows at the side of the van made it nearly impossible to see anybody sitting at the back as long as the van was in motion, the street was so packed with people that we should have to crawl along, often stopping, and then people would inevitably look in through the little back window and see an Arab crouching on the floor.

I was therefore obliged to turn the car around and retreat. But the same problem confronted us at whatever barrier we presented ourselves, for the police said that unofficial Jewish searchers were now stationed just inside the police barriers, waiting to search cars for themselves.

After thinking the matter over, the only way seemed to be to drive to Damascus Gate, where all the excitement was and where the explosion had taken place, and from there through the Arab quarter to the RAF (Royal Air Force) zone, which was strictly guarded and not open to the public. I had no pass for this zone, but trusted that the British guards would take pity on our predicament and allow us to drive through their zone, which would lead us straight into the street where our hospital was. We were stopped, of course, near the scene of the explosion, by very excited Arab searchers, but the presence of an Arab man hiding in the back and being carried to safety was, under the circumstances, highly in my favor, and we were allowed to pass.

When we reached the RAF zone and explained the position, the officer on duty at the barricade kindly allowed us through, and with intense relief we finally found ourselves in the quiet, enclosed haven of the hospital compound. It was now quite obvious that I could never again drive Assad through the Jewish area and past the barricades, even if he had been willing to risk it. The poor man was utterly terrified and insisted at once on being allowed to return to his village.

On December 15, a number of missionaries were obliged to leave their homes on Deir Abu Tor (the hill of Caiaphas's palace). It adjoined the main Bethlehem road and was right in the southern Arab sector. This hill was a convenient center from which Arabs could snipe at passing buses and cars, and the missionaries were therefore forced to leave and find somewhere else to settle. Two came to stay on the hospital compound, my friend Lilly[2] being one of them. Others decided to leave the country altogether, until conditions became more settled.

After their departure, Deir Abu Tor became notorious as an Arab terrorist stronghold. Later on, some of the bitterest fighting took place there as the Arabs sought to hold the position, and when the Jews finally wrested it from them, to regain it. The homes of the little missionary colony were then shelled to pieces. Mr. and Mrs. Shelley, both over eighty and veterans of the country, together with their faithful maid, were the only people who were allowed to remain. They went through incredible dangers until, months later, the Jewish Hagana forces evacuated them to a safer area.

On December 19 a young Hebrew Christian from Tel Aviv, not realizing the desperate tension in Jerusalem, was caught by Arabs near the border and taken to Jaffa Gate. There he was shot at and wounded but managed to escape to the mission compound. A rabble crowd of about a hundred then collected in the compound, demanding that he should be handed over to them. But a member of the staff had hurriedly phoned to the police, who arrived before the man was discovered, and clearing the courtyard, carried him safely away to the hospital.

From this time on, the van was in constant use for moving missionaries, friends, and their belongings. There was no bus, taxi, or truck communication between the Arab and Jewish quarters, and those who had to move could find no transport. People rang up from all over the city, apologetically explaining that there was no transport of any kind, and asking if I could possibly move this or fetch that. Patients had to be driven home, people were smuggled from area to area, and every day the hospital supplies had to be fetched. There was little enough time for housekeeping in the ordinary sense of the word, but the faithful Arab maids carried on the work with great loyalty and efficiency.

On December 26, after the bustle and excitement of celebrating Christmas at the hospital was over, I had a precious, free afternoon and I drove off alone in the van, with a picnic tea, to a quiet hillside on the outskirts of Jewish Jerusalem. I went down a rough track till I was just out of sight of the houses. It was too cold to sit outside, so I moved to the seat in the back of the van and, wrapping myself warmly in a blanket, prepared myself for the luxury of a quiet prayer afternoon in the open country.

Presently there was a distant bang, as though some kind of heavy artillery had been fired—not a rifle shot, but something louder and duller. Almost immediately afterwards something hit the ground beside the van with a heavy thud. *Is that only an explosion at one of the stone quarries,* I asked myself doubtfully, *or can it be that someone is firing in this direction?*

I leaned forward to look out of the window. The hillside on which the van was parked sloped steeply down to a deep and narrow valley, and another hill rose abruptly on the other side. On the brow of this opposite hill was a fair-sized Arab village named Deir Yassin, exactly facing the Jewish suburb of Beit Hakerem. Both hills were bare of trees, and in the clear air I could plainly see an Arab boy leading his goats across the rocky slope opposite me and hear him calling to them. Even as I looked, a puff of smoke spurted out from a spot just below the village, then another reverberation. The next moment something struck the van, which was facing the village broadside on, and ricocheted off again. With a curious feeling in my stomach, I realized that somebody was indeed firing from across the valley and that I and the van were the target!

Happily, I must have been almost out of range, for the missile rebounded harmlessly. But it was a nasty few minutes. I saw men moving on the opposite hillside, as though to improve their range, and with my heart in my mouth, I clambered over into the driver's seat and fumbled for the starter. It was necessary to back the van along the track to a slightly wider space and then turn and face her uphill. Expecting every moment that a third shot would come, I miscalculated the distance, and to my horror, felt both wheels start to slide over the edge. It was a dreadful moment, and I prayed desperately for help. I jammed on the brakes and accelerated anxiously; to my relief the car jerked forward, and I got her facing up the hill and away.

It was quite obvious that the time had come when one could no longer retire with impunity even to the outskirts of Jewish Jerusalem. We were passing into a state of siege.

From that time, the area in which we could move around seemed to shrink steadily and inexorably.

By the end of December more and more of our friends were preparing to leave Palestine, for Great Britain had decided to give up the mandate, and after that nobody knew what would happen. It was naturally very sad indeed to part with so many friends and fellow missionaries, but those of us who hoped to remain began to draw closer together than ever before.

On December 30 we heard the awful news that forty-one Jews had been killed at the oil refineries in Haifa, and scores more had been wounded. Their Arab fellow workers had suddenly fallen upon them and knifed and beaten them to death.

The last day of the year was marked for us at the hospital by a particularly tragic happening. Dr. Simon, one of the best-loved Jewish doctors who attended patients in our hospital, was murdered in cold blood while visiting an Arab patient in the still partly mixed suburb of Katamon.

These and other dreadful happenings made it clear that it was no longer safe for Jews and Arabs to work together anywhere. Therefore public departments, posts, banks, etc., all began to divide, with one section in the Arab areas and one in the Jewish. Partition seemed to be becoming more and more a horrifying reality. The city was indeed divided against itself.

2 *Barricades and Outrages*

The last night of 1947 arrived. There was no possibility of attending a Watch Night Service, for no one ventured out after dark, and generally there was a curfew. I woke just before midnight to hear the church bells ringing all over the Holy City, but they were quickly drowned by a tremendous outburst of shooting. For an hour I kept watch with the Lord, thinking back over the past year with all its many tests and difficulties, its wonderful happenings and many mercies. And I offered myself to him afresh, praying that I might be fitted for whatever the future held, and usable in the way that he should choose.

The guns rattled fiercely, disturbing the sleep of Jerusalem's citizens. And the verse that he gave as his promise for the New Year was, "Instead of the thorn shall come up the fir tree, and instead of the brier shall come up the myrtle tree: and it shall be to the LORD for a name, for an everlasting sign that shall not be cut off" (Isa. 55:13).

It looked as though there would be more than enough thorns and briers to embitter the coming year, but his strength and support, his grace and loving kindness, would surely outweigh them all.

On January 5, there was a wild storm all night long, and at 4:00 A.M. there was a prolonged thunderclap. As it died away, a terrific explosion occurred. The Stern Gang had blown up Semiramis Hotel in Katemon, a center of the Arab Higher Committee. We heard later on the radio that six people had been killed and at least fifteen more were buried under the ruins.

The weather now began to add to the sorrows and distresses of the population. Bitterly cold, wet weeks set in. Already many houses and most shops were without windows, for explosions had become commonplace, while the shortage of kerosene, Jerusalem's main fuel for heating and cooking, was becoming very acute.

At this time, Jewish terrorists seemed able to carry about and plant explosives almost with impunity. They were seldom caught, one great difficulty being that the police and military could never obtain cooperation from the population in arresting the terrorists. People either looked upon them as heroic patriots, or else they were desperately afraid of vengeance and reprisals if they dared bear witness against them. Certainly the large majority of Jerusalem's Jewish population deplored violence and terror, but it was simply not safe to take any part in bringing the terrorists to justice. Later on when these extremist groups had apparently succeeded in their avowed intention of forcing Great Britain to relinquish the mandate, more people began to feel that the state of Israel must use force and violence to deliver itself from its enemies.

On rare occasions the perpetrators of violence, by some accident or mishap, were caught. It happened once that a gentleman was driving himself to an appointment and, being a little late, was exasperated by a taxi driving very slowly just ahead. He accelerated, and in defiance of the rules, cut in at a crossroads. The taxi was forced against a traffic island with a great jerk, the door opened, and five men sprang out. As the car that had cut in dashed hurriedly forward, a tremendous explosion rocked the street. The taxi, which was full of explosives, was blown to pieces. Two of the terrorists were shot, and the other three were captured.

Although all direct passages between the Arab and Jewish areas were now closed, one zone remained in the middle of Jerusalem as a military area. In order to enter it, one had to possess a special permit. This zone contained the YMCA buildings, the King David Hotel and the Terra Santa boys' school. Passing through, one came to the so-called German colony where all British civilians had lived for a year in a protected zone. A second "gate" opened into the Jewish area, a third into the Arab. This military zone now became the hospital's lifeline.

Being British and a member of a hospital, I was granted the necessary pass and was able to drive through this neutral zone. It was a very long and roundabout route and used up a great deal of precious gasoline, but in those days one went incredible distances in order to reach friends who lived perhaps only a few streets away. When the mandate was finally given up and all connection between the two parts of

Jerusalem ceased, the following, quite possibly true, story was told: A journalist in the Arab area wanted to get into the Jewish area of Jerusalem. In order to do this, he drove from the Old City to Transjordan. From there he flew to Syria, then on to Cyprus and Italy, and from thence by air to Haifa. From Haifa he went to Tel Aviv by car, then up the so-called "Burma Road," and so back into the Jewish side of Jerusalem. This was a journey that in the ordinary way he could have accomplished by boarding a bus at Jaffa Gate and alighting two minutes later, higher up the street in the middle of the Jewish shopping center. No wonder "foreign" inhabitants thought wistfully of the rejected proposal for making Jerusalem an international city.

Even in the early weeks of the New Year, I was obliged, in the course of a return journey, to pass barricades no less than twelve times whenever I went to do hospital shopping in the well-stocked Arab market in the Old City. Besides these official barricades, all sorts of individuals armed with guns would suddenly step into the road at unexpected places and demand to search the van. Of course I always stopped immediately and encouraged them to do so, as it was good to have it openly demonstrated that I never carried explosives.

I must say at once that I never received anything but courtesy and friendliness at the Jewish barricades, even though at this time Britain was becoming looked upon more and more as an enemy. At the military barricades, of course, I was treated as a compatriot; and at the Arab barricades, where as a rule the guards could not read, I was generally treated with goodwill.

My blue van quickly became recognized at all the barricades, and as long as the same guards were on duty it was not too difficult. But every week or so they were changed, and then one had to begin all over again disarming suspicion and persuading them to let me pass. Negotiating the barricades became progressively difficult as the situation became more and more strained, but I felt I made many pleasant friends. The daily trips were always rather an adventure and sometimes definitely nerve-racking, depending on the state of my conscience and the kind of freight I had with me.

This seems a suitable moment in which to introduce Charles, a curly black-and-white dog, hardly bigger than a cat, bequeathed to me by a family leaving for England. He was the most loving little companion possible and could not bear me out of his sight. He looked upon the van and everything else that I had as his own particular property. I never went out without him. He was a most useful asset at the barriers and created a friendly atmosphere. He was far too small to sit on the seat and look out the window, so he stood on his hind legs and stuck out his head, his little black ears streaming in the wind.

It was interesting to watch his demeanor at the different barricades. With the Hagana he was polite but slightly aloof. At the British barricades all the guards naturally spoke to Charles before bothering about me, and he allowed himself to be petted and stroked in a condescending fashion. At the sight of an Arab guard in a red headdress, with gun in his hand, advancing towards the van, Charles would withdraw his head. When the man stooped down and put his face to the window to look inside, he would leap forward in a frenzy of indignation, with a bark far too large for his small body. If it were a new guard, the man, at this sudden onslaught, would leap back as though he had been shot, amid delighted roars of laughter from his companions.

Such a ridiculously small piece of bristling fur and furious bark seldom failed to raise a good-natured laugh, and the blue van with Charles's small face and waving ears protruding from the window became one of the recognized phenomena of Jerusalem. There were occasions when his presence saved me from embarrassing, perhaps dangerous, situations. More than once, when I did not want unofficial searchers to look in the van, Charles would leap towards the face trying to peer in the window like a small fury. As the man stepped back startled, I would smile cheerfully and say, "Oh, I beg your pardon; do excuse him," and thankfully drive off before he could recover himself.

In other parts of the country, the roads were becoming more and more dangerous for travel. We heard of the finding of thirty-five Jewish bodies between Jaba and Saris, in the Beisan district. In the Hebron area there were constant attacks against the isolated settlements in the Etz-Zion groups. The settlers defended themselves bravely, but they were solitary and small units in that large district. On the Lydda-Wilhelma Road, a bypass to Haifa, Jewish cars had been fired on and passengers murdered. What later came to be called "The Battle of the Roads" was already in full swing.

At 11:00 P.M. on February 2, we were all aroused by a terrible explosion. The housekeeper's bedroom was at the top of the hospital, and I hurried to the flat roof. Eastward, and quite near to us, there was a blazing fire and dense clouds of flame-lit smoke billowed up into the black sky. The next morning we heard that very powerful explosives had blasted the offices of the *Palestine Post*, the most widely read English-language paper in the country. For months past, this paper, in common with all other Jewish papers, had been criticizing the British Mandatory Government, and in particular the British police force. Immediately it became known that the paper's premises had been wrecked, and the outrage was blamed upon the police as a supposed reprisal. Anti-British feeling in those days was growing by leaps and bounds, and this added fuel to the flame.

The demolishing of the *Palestine Post* offices was not the worst part of the outrage. The explosives had been so powerful that they had wrecked the whole block, and besides the people who had been killed, many families had been made homeless in that bitterly cold February weather. Also the nearby Jewish first aid post had been wrecked, and one or two of their ambulances destroyed. As they had nowhere to carry on their noble and increasingly necessary work, and as our own hospital was already nearly empty, we were able to offer them the large outpatient department. They moved to the hospital compound at once and parked their ambulances under the trees.

On February 22, a very cold, dark Sunday morning, I was sitting in my turret room. All night long the wind had been rattling the tiny door that opened onto the roof and whistling through the tiny window. Outside, all was dark and forlorn; inside, by very contrast, it was cozy and cheerful. On Sundays we breakfasted at 7:00 A.M. instead of 6:30 A.M., and I was still enjoying my early quiet time. The lamp shone cheerfully on the crimson eiderdown and a tray with the early morning tea things. Charles was fast asleep on a chair beside the bed. It all seemed peaceful and secure and a happy beginning to a Sunday, always the red-letter day of the week with its quiet hours in church and fellowship with others.

At 6:30 A.M., without warning, there was a terrifying roar. The next instant, out of the darkness, rushed such a blast that seemed to shake the hospital to its foundations. The turret room rocked, the roof door flew open, the mirror fell from the wall, and from all directions came the sound of shattering glass and loud crashes. For one petrified second I could not move, then hurried on to the roof. In the first faint glimmer of dawn an immense wall of dust was visible, billowing up into the sky, apparently close at hand.

I ran downstairs to the first floor, and it looked as though the occupants of all the rooms had been hurtled by the blast into the corridor, where, herded together, they were comparing notes of the damage in their rooms. Curtains had been torn from windows, carpets rolled up, though in the same room a vase of flowers on the central table still stood intact. Floors were heaped with broken glass, locks had been wrenched from doors as they burst open, windows in all the wards had been shattered to pieces, and tiles had been torn from the roofs.

But what were these minor damages compared to the wreckage at the site of the explosion? Ambulances and cars were already dashing into the compound with their loads of wounded and dead while weeping people hurried from hospital to hospital, looking for their missing friends.

A little later we heard what had happened. A truck full of explosives had been parked outside the Atlantic Hotel in Ben Yehuda Street. It had been accompanied by men wearing uniforms of British police, who had ridden off in a jeep and left the truck behind. A few seconds later it had exploded, shattering to pieces the Atlantic Hotel and four whole blocks of houses.

It was a crowded area, and homes from end to end of the street had been damaged, while streets in every direction had been littered and blocked with broken glass, tiles, and rubble. Fifty people, many of them children, had been killed, and scores more wounded and made homeless. At that early hour of the morning, most of them had been still sleeping peacefully in bed and so had been quite unable to escape. A number of the people made homeless in this appalling tragedy were refugees from the houses that had already been demolished with the *Palestine Post* offices only three weeks earlier.

This was, by far, the worst explosion that had occurred in Jerusalem except for the blowing up of the King David Hotel in 1946, when Jewish terrorists, disguised as milkmen, had rolled milk barrels filled with powerful explosives into the cellars under the wing that housed the secretariat. This had been done in broad daylight, at a time when the building was crowded. Scores of people had been buried under the ruins, and more than a hundred had lost their lives.

The fact that the perpetrators of this horrible outrage in Ben Yehuda Street had worn the uniforms of British policemen, and when challenged on arrival at the Jewish barricades had answered in English and used their authority as supposed British police to drive through without being searched, led the whole Jewish community to conclude at once that the outrage had been committed by bona fide policemen. Therefore the community believed that those who were there to preserve law and order had thus diabolically abused their power.

It was in vain for the authorities to point out that nearly all Jewish terrorist activities and violence had been carried out by men wearing stolen British uniforms, and that this trick had been the means by which extremists on both sides had succeeded in committing some of their most violent anti-British activities. The community, roused and infuriated by the terrible sufferings inflicted on so many innocent civilians and children, rose as one man and demanded the removal of all British military police from the Jewish area. The streets were once again thronged by seething crowds, and self-instituted groups of young people formed barricades and searched anyone who looked like a foreigner. A warning was issued that any British policeman found in the Jewish area from that time on would be shot. The authorities therefore decided to evacuate all British forces from the Jewish area of Jerusalem, leaving the maintaining of law and order to the Jewish police.

It was a sad drive to church that tragic Sunday morning, through streets littered with rubble and thronged with a mourning, infuriated population. It was a sad and terrible contrast to the jubilant throng that had so exultingly celebrated partition three months before. Ben Yehuda Street was cordoned off, and crowds were working desperately to dig out the buried families, while others searched despairingly for any sign of their loved ones.

It was these awful hatreds that made Palestine so dreadful. The country seemed to burn from end to end with hate — hate of the Jews, hate of the British, hate of the Arabs. Violence had bred vengeance and hate, as it always does, and fierce desire to see the other side suffer. It felt at times as though the Holy City reeked with some awful miasma from hell.

Next door to our hospital was the big Mustashfe police billet. When we reached home after the afternoon service, we found the British police were evacuating bag and baggage; and as we arrived, men began firing at the billet from all the neighboring rooftops. Evidently the terrorists meant to have one last fling. The battle that ensued was terrific. Most of the police had already left, and the remaining truckloads were lining up in the billet yard when the attack began at 5:00 P.M.

For two hours the besieged police fired back in all directions. Darkness had fallen, but still the rifles cracked and Sten guns rattled and bullets whizzed past our windows and ricocheted off the walls. We herded together in inner passages or sat on the floor, out of range of the windows. For on a previous occasion when the billet was attacked, no less than fifty bullets had been picked up in one of the empty wards, the police claiming that some of the terrorists had actually hidden in the hospital grounds and fired from there.

At last, at 7:00 P.M., after two hours of ceaseless battle, we heard the noise of approaching army tanks, and then a terrific outbreak of thunderous firing. The rooftop shooting died down as the military arrived on the scene in considerable strength, and the last of the British police were convoyed out of the Jewish area.

The next morning, when we looked out of the hospital windows, we saw that the Union Jack had gone from the flagstaff of the next-door billet and the blue and white Jewish flag fluttered in its place.

3

Closing the Hospital

The New Year had certainly begun with sufficient difficulties. The very first day the three remaining menservants at the hospital came to give notice, saying, quite truly, that it was too dangerous for them to remain in the Jewish area. It is difficult to run a hospital with no men helpers; there is so much heavy carrying to do, and Jewish labor, even if we could have secured it, was prohibitively expensive. So the departure of our three men simply hastened the crisis we were inevitably reaching in connection with the hospital.

Except for a few chronic cases in two of the wards, we had no new patients coming to us. Of course, this meant a drastic falling off in income, so that it was quite impossible to maintain our big staff. It seemed obvious that the situation would deteriorate still more. When in a few months the British Mandate was to end, real war seemed inevitable. Then our Arab maidservants would certainly have to leave, and already all Jewish nurses had been called up to work in Jewish hospitals.

The food situation was becoming more and more precarious, and I wondered how much longer it would be possible to feed so large a family. When I informed the doctor, who was ill in bed, that our menservants were leaving almost immediately, it became evident that under the circumstances it was no longer possible to run the hospital. Sometime in the future, tragic as it seemed, we would have to close it.

By the middle of January it was definitely settled that we were to close the hospital. It was decided that we would hand it over temporarily to the Jewish people to help them in their time of need, for the famous Jewish Hadassah Hospital, on Mount Scopus, was already becoming inaccessible.

The Jewish Hadassah Hospital was right outside Jerusalem near the Hebrew University and could not be reached except by passing through the Arab area, which was quite impossible without military escort. Electrically detonated mines along the road to Mount Scopus were constantly exploding under buses, cars, and military vehicles, or bombs were hurled into the buses on their way to the hospital or the university.

The government hospital was inside the Arab area, and the two main hospitals in the Jewish area were quite unable to cope with the needs of the whole population. The mission hospital, therefore, was to become temporarily the Hadassah Hospital in Jerusalem. In this way it was felt that, although the mission could no longer carry on its medical work and witness, the hospital would still serve the Jewish people.

We were to hand it over, through the International Red Cross, to the Hadassah authorities on March 19, retaining one of the doctor's houses, which stood in its own garden. This was to be kept as a mission house, the upper flat being used by those of the staff who were willing and able to remain, and the lower flat to be used as the girls' school. This had been reopened on the hospital compound on January 12 under almost impossible difficulties, including lack of space, lack of experienced staff, lack of equipment, and the appallingly cold weather with complete lack of fuel.

On March 11 one of the American consulate cars drove into the courtyard of the Jewish agency in Jerusalem. The driver was a well-known and trusted Arab, and the consulate car was allowed to park in the courtyard as usual. American policy was held in high favor by the Jews, and no one thought of suspecting the consulate car, nor searching it. The driver got out and, mingling with the crowds, disappeared. A few moments later another heavy explosion rocked Jerusalem, as the American consulate car, standing inside the closely guarded precincts of the Jewish agency, exploded into a thousand pieces.

The Jewish agency was the most carefully guarded building in Jerusalem. Being the headquarters of the Jewish authorities, everyone knew that if it were possible to get near it, this was the first place the Arabs would choose to destroy. The most minute precautions were taken to preserve it from danger. But who would ever conceive that an American consulate car, belonging to Israel's greatest ally, could be used as a vehicle for explosives? Evidently the Arab driver had been heavily bribed or deemed it a deed of highest patriotism. He disappeared completely and, as far as we know, was never seen again.

The Jewish Agency building is too massively built to be wrecked by a mere carload of explosives. But this daring attack resulted in the death of eleven people, while thirty-three others were injured seriously and fifty-five slightly wounded. Considerable damage was done to one wing of the building. Besides this, a great many houses were slightly damaged by the explosion. We and many others lost more of our windows, which had only just, at long last, been repaired after the Ben Yehuda explosion. The wintry weather made this constant loss of windows very trying indeed. There were torrential hailstorms and, a few days later, a heavy fall of snow. We ate our meals in the dining room with all the shutters closed and the lights on. It was cold and dreary in the extreme.

We were by now in the throes of closing down the hospital, making inventories, storing away all such furniture and equipment as the Hadassah did not need, and cleaning up. On March 19 the hospital closed, and all of our Palestinian staff left. There had been a heavy fall of snow, and this added to our difficulties as we slipped and skidded about the grounds and on the streets. Fiendish little boys lurked by the wayside, hurling snowballs with stones in them at the cars. The Hadassah were already beginning to move in their equipment, and altogether that last week the staff was hard pressed. The girls' school, in Ruth's charge, was still continuing in one of the wards, and there were a number of Hebrew Christian refugees who had had to leave their homes in the non-Jewish areas and had no place of asylum other than the mission compound.

When the cleaning up was all finished and the faithful maidservants driven to their homes in Bethlehem and

Beit Jala, the doctor and all the British staff moved down to the mission hostel just inside Jaffa Gate. They were to leave for England in the course of the next few days. I moved to the hostel too; but as I still had the British zone pass, I was able to drive to the hospital compound almost daily, carry supplies for the school staff and the Hebrew Christians, and lay in some stores for such staff as might remain when the mandate ended and Jewish Jerusalem would almost certainly be completely besieged.

The last Sunday that we all met in the mission church before the doctor and sisters left, I glanced round the little congregation. Nearly all were missionaries or British police and officials. There were only four of us who were not expecting to leave the country. Come what may, I knew that God meant me to remain, though I did not in the least know what was his next plan for me. But of course he would make it plain and show whether I was to remain in the Arab or Jewish areas.

All of the services of those last few weeks before the British left were very precious indeed. We were soon going to separate, and those who expected to remain were few. No one could foresee what the future would bring, but almost certainly it was battle and the shadow of death. But as we gathered at the prayer meetings or met in the church, we had an ever-deepening sense of being one little family of God's children in the midst of threatening billows and fast-approaching tempest. As one after another left and our numbers were sifted down, and as the constant farewells were made, the sense of union deepened and we seemed to hear the Lord's own words, "Fear not, little flock; for it is your Father's good pleasure to give you the kingdom" (Luke 12:32).

By the time the hospital was closed, most of the missionaries in Jerusalem had left. All mission schools were closed except the little one on the hospital compound. It seemed as though, at least temporarily, all regular missionary institutional work had come to an end.

On March 24 our doctor flew to England, and three days later the sisters also left in a convoy with other British civilians. On March 20 the United States had announced its opinion that the partition plan was proving impossible to implement. This was hailed as a great victory for the Arabs, as it would mean no Jewish state. Once again the Jewish people were roused to bitter opposition and to insist more strongly that the decision of the United Nations in favor of partition must be carried out. The already deplorable situation was acutely aggravated, and everything plunged again into the melting pot and into further uncertainty.

4

The Battle
of the Roads

A few days after the Ben Yehuda outrage and before the hospital closed, the opportunity arrived for me to spend a weekend away from the hospital—the first time this had been possible since I had become the housekeeper five months before.

One Friday afternoon in the first week of March, I joyfully got out the blue van, and in company with Brookie and our two dogs, we set off for Tel Aviv. Travel was already hazardous in the extreme, especially at such points where one had to cross over from Arab to Jewish territory, or vice-versa. The main road to Jaffa–Tel Aviv left Jerusalem from the Jewish area, so of course no Arab traffic could use it. But almost as soon as it left the city it was in Arab territory, with Arab villages all along the route, whose inhabitants were well aware that any vehicles upon the road must be Jewish and therefore natural targets for shooting practice.

This road was Jewish Jerusalem's one precarious life-line, and unfortunately it was terribly vulnerable, for it wound in and out among the mountains and through narrow valleys. From Arab villages on the heights overlooking it, snipers were already taking a dreadful toll, and it was becoming increasingly difficult to bring supplies to the city.

We, of course, did not dare to use this death trap of a road, but rather slipped through the British zone into the Arab area and got on the main road to Ramallah, from where a new military road led down to the plain right through Arab territory. It was wonderful to be out in the country again after being shut up so long amid streets and houses; it seemed half a lifetime since I had been among the olive trees and enjoyed unobstructed views of mountain and sea. It was real March weather: black clouds, sudden storms, and then short intervals of brilliant sunshine. The countryside was beautiful, fresh, and fragrant after the rain, its changing colors looking like a newly painted picture.

There were Arab road checks at frequent intervals, but everyone was friendly. After a most enjoyable run down the mountains, we joined the main road near Latrun and around 4:00 P.M. approached a sandy track that was now the only route to the Jewish city, as the main road went on into Arab Jaffa. We wondered if there would be snipers hiding behind a cactus hedge, ready to riddle us with bullets as soon as we left the main road, for we knew that during the last few days, cars turning off onto this track had been fired at from close range.

There were no snipers. Instead the road suddenly became a scene of great activity. British tanks were drawn up at the side, and armed soldiers were on duty as guards. Right across the entrance to the sandy track, there was a barricade guarded by Jewish soldiers.

When we drew up at this barricade and explained that we wanted to go to Tel Aviv and then produced our British passports, we were told that it was impossible for us to go any farther. Since the Ben Yehuda explosion two or three days before, the Jewish authorities had determined to bar all Britishers from entering Tel Aviv without special permits. We, of course, did not have these permits, not having heard of the new regulation.

We pleaded eloquently the difficult plight we were in, two hapless women on a dangerous road as night fell, and one of them, a citizen of Tel Aviv, thus debarred from reaching her home. It would soon be curfew, and then what would happen to us? At last they put a guard in the van and told us to drive along the track to the next barricade and see what the area officer would decide.

At the next barricade, we were very politely arrested. The van was searched from top to bottom, and all the suitcases were ransacked for possible explosives. A special cupboard had been built into the van for holding our stores of literature, and when this was unlocked, it so happened that a number of Arabic Gospels and tracts fell off the shelf. There was dead silence for a moment as Arabic leaflets settled all over the floor. Then one searcher hastily collected them and said, "I am afraid we must examine these," and walked rapidly off.

A crowd of Jewish Hagana soldiers now stood round the van, and I explained that I had the same leaflets and books in Hebrew, as well as Hebrew New Testaments, and I should be so happy to give them to anyone who was interested. Instantly there were requests from all sides, and I was kept busy distributing literature in other languages as well as in Hebrew.

Presently the men who had carried off the Arabic literature returned, and with an amused smile said, "Yes indeed, this is Christian literature and not Arab or British propaganda." We were then courteously, but firmly, requested to leave the van and were taken to a guard room, where we sat for nearly two hours while the guards phoned here and there asking if we were to be permitted to enter Tel Aviv.

Night fell, dark and very wet, and when at last the hoped-and-prayed-for permission was granted and a car with two guards arrived to escort us to the mission house, we drove through thunder, lightning, and torrential rain along inky black streets. They were quite empty, for there was a curfew because of continuous sniping on the borders of Jaffa–Tel Aviv.

At last with great relief we drew up before the mission house. In another moment the door had opened, and Laurie[3] came running out through the pouring rain and scrambled into the van to greet us. She had only just been able to get back from England. She and I had been evacuated in 1947 with the rest of the British women and children, under Operation Polly. I had returned to help at the hospital, and now, at last, she had been able to get back to beloved Palestine.

The next day Laurie and I drove off to spend the weekend at her home right out in the country, on the Plain of Sharon. It is impossible to describe the sense of freedom and delight with which I found myself able to wander about freely after being shut up for so many months in the city. It was wild tulip time down there on the plain, and protected by

Wellington boots, we splashed through bogs, along miry footpaths, through dripping orange groves, and we gathered armfuls of beautiful scarlet tulips till we could carry no more. Charles went nearly mad with joy. He chased imaginary "rabbits" and dived down "burrows," and we all three abandoned ourselves to the rapture of wandering over the countryside.

At length, as dusk fell, we started home and only then noticed the blackness of the sky. Then began such a downpour that we were nearly blinded. Weighed down with our loads of tulips, we waded home. Poor little Charles at times nearly had to swim. When we got home, he was so coated in the reddish-yellow soil of the plain that he looked like a bedraggled fox cub, with no trace of a black-and-white curly-haired dog about him. To his horror, on arrival at the house this distressing situation was deplorably worsened by his being immediately plunged into a tub of cold water and soused from head to foot before being allowed inside the house!

That night we lay in bed listening to the storm and wind and peals of thunder and the loud howling of packs of jackals all around the house. These were all good, familiar sounds, and I loved to hear them. No shooting, no explosions, no rumbling and rattling of ambulances, no sirens, and no police loudspeakers. Charles, warmly wrapped in a dry towel and a blanket, slumbered blissfully on the foot of the bed and dreamed of sandy tunnels in the orange groves and didn't even deign to answer the jackals.

The next morning Laurie helped me to push the van out of the miry yard. As we said good-bye to each other, we both realized that it might be many months before we could meet again. The Palestine we had known and loved for so long was changing into something new and unpredictable. Who could tell if the old freedom would ever come again or what would evolve out of the present maelstrom. One thing seemed certain: Difficult and sad times lay ahead. The situation would worsen before it could improve. We could not see what was coming or even imagine it. But of one thing we could be sure: All of God's promises still held good. He had granted us this time together that we might strengthen one another's hands, and now, though we must go our separate ways, nothing could bar the way into his presence. We both had access to him.

So I went back up the mountain road to Ramallah. The weather had cleared, and I ate my midmorning sandwiches in an olive grove, where cyclamen and scarlet anemones grew lavishly among the rocks. And so laden with spring treasures, Charles and I came, at midday, back to battered Jerusalem.

Two weeks later, on March 19, when we closed the hospital, one Arab ward maid who had been there for fifteen years was left with nowhere to go, but the CMS hospital at Gaza very kindly offered to take her as a ward maid there. Owing to the chaotic conditions of road transport, there seemed no way of getting her and her belongings down to Gaza. In the end it fell to my lot to drive her there by a long, roundabout route which was quite new to me.

The necessity for trying to remain in one territory without passing into any part of the other meant that the distance of most journeys was tripled or quadrupled. Even so, there were so many Jewish settlements in the Arab area, and still more Arab villages in the Jewish area, that it was generally impossible to avoid passing isolated danger spots where snipers might be hidden. On this occasion we had first to drive to Ramallah, a distance of nine miles, along an Arab main road, with two lonely Jewish settlements lying close beside it—first Neve Ya'acov and then Atarot, which was close beside the small Kalandia Airport.

Just after passing Damascus Gate, we found a long convoy of Arab buses and armored cars lined at the roadside. A guard stopped us and told us to join the convoy, as there was sniping somewhere ahead, and it was not safe to travel to Ramallah alone. He said the convoy might leave in about an hour's time, and added, "You will be quite safe if you travel with our Arab Army escort, and you may see some Jews shot dead."

This more than convinced me not to wait. The last thing I, as a Christian and a pacifist, wanted to do was to join any military escort, whether Arab, Jewish, or British, that might be constrained to use force or violence. I told the guard that we had a long journey ahead and could not afford to wait for the convoy. We would drive on a little ways and see if perhaps by now the road was safe. If not, we would wait further on. We saw two British policemen near the American colony and stopped to ask them if the road ahead was safe, as we were then close to the notorious Sheikh Jaraeh quarter, where Arab sniping was constant. They said as far as they knew all was quiet, so without further hesitation I drove on and out into the open country.

A few miles out of Jerusalem, the main road abruptly turns around a low, jutting hill that completely hides the Jewish settlement of Neve Ya'acov. Once around this corner, the road runs beside the settlement and goes zigzagging down a hill to a wide gully and a hairpin bend across a culvert and then straightens out the other side.

We had seen no traffic on the road since we left Jerusalem. As we approached this jutting hill, I slowed down in order to turn the sharp corner, after which the road ran beside Neve Ya'acov. There were red crosses on the van, quite plain enough to be visible in the streets of a town, but probably not easily distinguishable from a hillside.

As we turned the corner and drove on beside the settlement, a bullet whistled past the front window. They were firing at us from close range and had missed by inches. My mind seemed to go icy cold with fear, but at the same time to become crystal clear. My first thought was, "The angel of the LORD encampeth round about them that fear him, and delivereth them" (Ps. 34:7). The words seemed to form themselves in my mind almost audibly. The next thought was, "They always aim at the driver or the tires. I must accelerate all I can." Then the second bullet passed so near it seemed it must have hit the back of the van, but once again it missed. The maid beside me was gasping with fright, my own heart was pounding and my hands were clammy. I heard myself praying aloud: "Dear Lord Jesus, do help us. Remember your promises. You know I must slow down at the hairpin bend or we shall dash into the gully. Don't let them shoot us there."

Accelerating with all my might, we sped giddily down the hillside towards the hairpin bend and the gully. We lurched across the culvert and out on to a straight stretch of road where we could race at full speed. Still the road lay before us, completely empty of traffic, and I realized we were rushing towards the second Jewish settlement, beside Kalandia Airport. It was visible from quite a distance, and as we came in sight of it, I began to tremble again and to slow down. Then we saw two khaki-clad figures lying flat on the ground beside the road, with their guns pointing away from us. Pulling up beside them, not sure if they were Jewish or British soldiers, I asked breathlessly, "Are they sniping from this settlement too?"

"No," they answered grimly, still with their guns trained on the road ahead. "You can go on."

We went on, therefore, rather like Christian in *Pilgrim's Progress* after he had heard that there were lions in the way. Accelerating at top speed, we sped like an arrow past the silent settlement on our left and turned round another hill. Here we had to pull up quickly, for as we turned the corner we found the road before us packed with vehicles. Arab men stepped out and held up their hands for us to stop. It was a convoy of cars, buses, and taxis on their way to Jerusalem from Ramallah, and they had been warned that Jewish snipers were holding the road. They said they had been waiting there for nearly an hour. They were amazed to see us appear from the Jerusalem direction and eagerly wanted to know if the military had cleared out the snipers' nest. We were obliged to reply in the negative, and they passed on the news, muttering and cursing with rage, and then wished us a safe journey.

So we went on our way, past numerous barricades and roadblocks, down the mountains, and across country, southwest towards Gaza, which we eventually reached about 3:00 P.M. In this area there were only three or four small, isolated Jewish settlements standing back some distance from the road. Even so, being in Arab territory, we eyed them askance, just as we would have dreaded passing Arab villages had we been in Jewish territory.

Early the next morning, resisting the hospitable entreaties of the staff to remain longer, I set out on the return journey with no company but the little dog, Charles. First I wanted to buy gasoline but discovered that there was none to be bought in the whole of Gaza, as the main road from the Haifa refineries lay right through Jewish territory. Fortunately, I thought, I still had enough to get me as far as Ramleh, where I hoped I might be able to refill.

A few miles out of Gaza we came to an army jeep drawn across the road and two taxis lining up behind it. The soldiers said briefly that fighting was going on further up the road and all traffic must wait. So Charles and I parked ourselves behind the taxis and obediently waited. A truck drew up behind us and then one or two more vehicles, but as the road turned a corner, I could not see how many more joined the line.

After about half an hour the jeep drove off, and we concluded that we could proceed. The two taxis and I got a good start and hurried off. But about a mile further on, I suddenly caught sight of a gas pump on the opposite side of the road, and, wonder of wonders, a man was operating it and evidently filling cans for an empty bus that stood beside the pump. I felt this was far too good an opportunity to miss. Here was gasoline, and who knew where else I would be able to buy it in the Arab area if I passed this pumping station.

Glancing in the mirror as I slowed down, I saw the armored truck close behind me and realized I had no time to cross the road to the pump. I therefore signaled to the truck to go on while I pulled up at the side of the road and waited for it to pass. It did so, and was followed by another and another, and to my amazement as I sat there, a whole convoy of armor-plated buses swept past me, one after the other. There must have been forty vehicles in the convoy, and they were all completely closed and bulletproof. My light van was the only unprotected vehicle among them all, as the two taxis had long since forged ahead and out of sight.

When the last bus had rumbled past with its invisible driver and passengers, I crossed the road and drew up beside the gas pump. Two men stood there and, without any greeting, eyed me with surly suspicion. I sensed something very curious, a strange feeling of danger. However, I produced my Arab pass and pleaded for fuel.

On perceiving the pass, the men's attitude changed slightly and became more friendly. They were busy filling cans, however, and seemed in a hurry, and I said I would wait.

I began to look about me. There was no house in sight, only the pumping station at the edge of the road. On either side stretched fields of waving green corn, waist high, and so vivid a green in the bright spring sunlight, they hardly seemed real. There were no other human beings in sight save the two surly men. I gazed idly at the empty bus, and had not even got as far as wondering why a completely empty bus was standing there, when I suddenly heard shouts. Looking up, I saw fifteen or sixteen men wading towards us through the waist-high green corn. I was really startled, and for a moment fearful, for I wondered if they were shouting so angrily at me. Where had they suddenly come from? A moment or two before, no one had been visible. And why was such a group of men walking in the field and trampling down the new corn in that unexpected fashion?

Just then another armor-plated bus came dashing along the road in the wake of the convoy, and as it passed us, shots rang out. The two men leaped towards the shelter of the pumping station, and in an instant the trampling figures in the field had fallen flat among the corn and were invisible. I was left standing quite alone by the pump, with my heart pounding, and beginning to wonder if I was in a dream.

The owner of the pump came back to me. "Here, get away as quickly as you can," he said roughly, and poured two gallons of gas into my tank. "This is no place for you."

"Who fired those shots?" I asked, "and what convoy was that which passed?"

"The Jewish convoy you were traveling with," he said grimly.

"A Jewish convoy!" I gasped. "Impossible. I came from Gaza this morning, and there were two Arab taxis just in front of me."

"We thought you were part of the convoy," he grunted. "Get home as fast as you can. No one ought to be out on the roads alone in times like these."

Then I realized that the convoy must have drawn up behind us as we waited at the roadblock, and my heart filled with thankfulness that God had caused me to stop at the pump and not to have to drive through miles of Arab territory, the only defenseless car in an armed Jewish convoy.

Still feeling startled and not at all understanding the position, and staring amazed at the men who had once more risen up in the cornfield and were now nearing the pump, I got into the van. And obeying the man's repeated injunction to leave at once, I drove off.

The car had gone perhaps a few hundred yards when, looking ahead, I saw another company of men also coming in from the green corn. But these men were coming slowly, in pairs, and between them they dragged heavy sagging objects. "They must be sacks of something," I told myself. "But why are they lugging sacks through a cornfield?" I began suddenly to feel as though I were in a nightmare. They had almost reached the road when I saw that they were not sacks that each couple supported but dead bodies.

They were very near me as I slowed down, and I felt sick
and did not know whether to turn back or not, whether the
battle was over or if I should run into it if I went on. Charles,
who had been hanging out of the window as usual, whim-
pered and shivered all over. Then he came and laid his head
on my knee and looked up at me trustfully, as if to say,
"Well, you are here, so it's all right." And I knew that must
be my own attitude. I lifted my heart to the Lord and said,
"You are here, Lord, so it's all right," and went on.

For miles I drove alone along that main road, determined
on one thing: I would drive alone at any cost and slow down
to allow any vehicles that might come along to pass me.
After what seemed like hours, I reached the side road that
was to lead me across country and thankfully left that hateful main road.

A little further on, a winter stream ran under a bridge,
and I stopped the van and took Charles down for a drink as
he looked so miserable and sick. An old *fellahin* came along
on his donkey and naturally stopped to find out who I was.
I told him what I had seen, and I suppose he saw from my
face how I was feeling. He got off his donkey, and with a
kindly smile that I shall always remember, he said, "Here,
take these," and passed me two oranges he had kept for his
own lunch. Somehow that kindly smile and action from a
complete stranger, an Arab peasant, comforted my heart,
and I drove on feeling that kindliness and friendliness did
still exist in what had suddenly become a nightmare country.

When I reached Ramallah, I asked anxiously about the
road past Neve Ya'acov and was told that there had been no
more sniping. By 3:00 P.M. I was back in Jerusalem, thankful indeed that the journey was over and for the Lord's wonderful protection. But it made me realize as nothing else the

desperate situation all over the country and what the papers and radio meant when they spoke daily of "the Battle of the Roads." For many weeks these things had been happening on all the roads, and often there had been ghastly battles. *How many more dead bodies*, I wondered drearily, *lay hidden in the green cornfields or were left in ditches and gullies?*

That same evening we were all gathered in the hostel lounge before supper. The room was buzzing with conversation, as the hostel was already filled to overflowing with Hebrew and Arab Christians who had been obliged to leave their homes. I was knitting peacefully on the sofa and thinking how pleasant it was to be back in the shelter of the compound and not exposed to the hazards of the roads.

Suddenly, without warning, at 6:30 P.M., a terrific explosion occurred. Two men who were sitting in front of the window were thrown into the middle of the room, and all over the compound we heard the sound of crashing glass.

In the darkness, by the light of torches and dim lamps, for nearly an hour we swept up the littered glass and made things as shipshape as possible. Heavy firing was going on all the time as Arabs attacked the outpost of Yemin Moshe, a Jewish suburb just outside the Jaffa Gate, which fronted Arab positions on the city wall. There was only a narrow valley between, and Yemin Moshe had to bear the brunt of Arab attacks, as from its position it was particularly vulnerable. But the Jews refused to evacuate it, and night after night for a long time to come we lay in bed listening to the firing on Yemin Moshe.

The next morning the radio announced that Arab troops had attacked a Jewish convoy on the way to relieve the defenders of Neve Ya'acov, the settlement that had been sniping at traffic on the Ramallah road. In revenge for this continued sniping, they had nearly wiped out the convoy.

Fourteen Jews had been killed and their bodies cut to pieces. After that, the British insisted that both the settlements should be evacuated, and the Ramallah road was left clear.

5 *Easter*

Behold the stone is rolled away,
And shining Ones have come to say,
"He is not here, he is risen,
He is not here, but is risen."

I woke on Easter Day at 5:00 A.M. It
was quite dark, and as usual, the guns
were firing, as they had been all night.
As I dressed I thought of Mary
Magdalene at the tomb, and the words
seemed to ache in my heart, that when
she got there "it was yet dark." How
dark the night seemed in Palestine this
Easter Day. When would the morning
come? Then, just as I finished dressing,
the sun rose, a fiery golden ball, breaking through the mist over the eastern
limit of Olivet. The risen sun after the
dark night; the loveliest symbol of our
risen Lord, rising with healing in his

wings. As surely as dawn follows night, he will come again and end this long night of the world's sorrow.

Although there was spasmodic shooting, Ruth and I drove to the Garden Tomb. It was just after 6:00 A.M. and there was no one there. We had the whole garden to ourselves. We separated, and I went to the seat on the mound that overlooks the green hill.

Easter was early this year, and Calvary was all in flower. It was green everywhere on the summit and all around, while mauve lace-like flowers blossomed on the rock face of the skull. A little peach tree was radiant with blossoms. It was mild and sunny, and I listened to him speaking about "the power of his resurrection" as I sat there for an hour near the hill, perhaps the one on which he died.

Just before we left the garden to return to the mission church for Communion, I went and knelt in the tomb. At that moment there was a heavy shell explosion near at hand, but in the rock cave it sounded muffled and unreal. The caretaker and his wife told us that all night long that area had been shelled, and they had taken shelter in the tomb. What a contrast it seemed. Destruction and death all night, and Easter morning with his message of victory over death.

Later on in the day we heard that Mildred Marston, one of the teachers at the girls' college, had been shot on her way to midmorning service at the cathedral. She and another member of the college staff had been walking along St. Paul's Road when there was a sudden burst of shooting. Mildred had received a bullet through the brain, while her companion had thrown herself on the ground and was unhurt. Both of them had been expecting to leave for England in a few days' time, as the girls' college had to close. Amid this sorrow there was comfort in the thought that she began this Easter Day in the earthly Jerusalem and finished it in the heavenly one with the multitudes of the redeemed who worship and adore him for the life that is forever and who share in the power of his resurrection.

Mildred Marston was buried the next day. It was wet and cold, but as we left the government hospital and drove to Mount Zion to the Protestant cemetery, the sun shone out in real spring fashion. It was still possible to drive to Zion Hill in the intervals when there was no fighting (though a week or two later this became quite impossible), and as we went up to the cemetery we looked across the narrow valley at battered Yemen Moshe. Standing in the cemetery among the trees and flowering shrubs, those loveliest of words were read,

"I beheld, and, lo, a great multitude, which no man could number, . . . stood before the throne, and before the Lamb, clothed with white robes, and palms in their hands, . . . They shall hunger no more, neither thirst any more; neither shall the sun light on them, nor any heat. For the Lamb which is in the midst of the throne shall feed them, and shall lead them unto living fountains of waters: and God shall wipe away all tears from their eyes" (Rev. 7:9, 16–17).

Mildred was the first of the missionary group to be killed. Miss Thompson, the welfare officer, was standing with us at the graveside. The next day she, too, was shot dead as she was driving to the government hospital at Beit Safafa and was buried beside Mildred.

When Easter was over, and as the busy life at the hospital was finished and there were a few days' breathing space for rest and change, I had an intense longing to get away somewhere quiet, alone, and away from all the coming and going to meet the Lord and learn from him what was his next plan for me. There had been no time or opportunity in those last hectic weeks to go apart with him, and I felt I simply did not know what his will was now that the hospital had closed. It looked as though the coming months would be full of difficulties, dangers, and strain, and there was need to receive his strength and grace in preparation.

It was clear that any change of scene must be somewhere in the Arab territory, not too far away from Jerusalem. A few weeks before, a very welcome invitation had come from the CMS hospital in Nablus, in the very heart of Palestine, and I could get there without leaving Arab territory. The posts and telegraphs were terribly disorganized, but I wrote to say I hoped to make the visit. On April 3 Charles and I started off in the van.

Since the trip to Gaza the week before, I had a great dread of making any journey, and the thought of again driving past Neve Ya'acov was most unnerving. Indeed I was so tormented by fear of snipers that I almost decided to accept the escort of a police car as far as Ramallah. As it was but a few days since Miss Marston and Miss Thompson had been shot, it was only the realization that I must get away to have some quiet days if I were to be prepared to face the coming months that kept me to my resolution of going to Nablus.

When I had agreed to go with a police car, which would give me protection, my distress of mind increased a hundredfold. In all of our years of visiting every single settlement and Arab village in Palestine, right through all the disturbances, we had always refused to ask for armed protection. Surely at this stage it could not be right either. I decided that I must not allow anything to frighten me into going with an armed escort, and at once my mind was at peace.

On the morning of my departure I read the great and comforting message in Ezra 8:22, 31:

"I was ashamed to require of the king a band of soldiers and horsemen to help us against the enemy in the way: because we had spoken unto the king, saying, 'The hand of our God is upon all them for good that seek him'; . . . And the hand of our God was upon us, and he delivered us from the hand of the enemy, and of such as lay in wait by the way."

Greatly encouraged by these verses, I set off alone, though my heart quailed as I turned that dreadful corner where once before they had sniped at us. But all was quiet, and once past Ramallah, the ride was pure joy from start to finish.

It was a very different trip from the ones to Tel Aviv and Gaza. I had no passenger with me to feel responsible for. There were mountains all around and an almost deserted road. It was my own part of the country where I had once lived. Over these same wild mountains running down the middle of Palestine, I had driven over endless rough tracks to visit and preach in Moslem villages.

It was early summer, but the country was unspeakably lovely and had not yet begun to look parched and dry. I stopped in the wilderness of the Valley of Thieves (a great place for bandits and holdups in my earlier years) to eat some sandwiches and drink a thermos of tea. The flowers were glorious—scarlet anemones, huge yellow daisies, and every olive tree was surrounded by a carpet of little purple flowerets.

By midday I reached the valley between Mount Gerizim and Mount Ebal, in the very heart of Palestine, and drove up to the gate of the mission hospital. Though not expected, I received the most loving welcome. My letter had not arrived, and my hostess explained that she thought no one would travel by that road as the sniping from Neve Ya'acov was so much dreaded. Only a few days before, their doctor was driving to Jerusalem to see about her passport before leaving for England. As she approached the settlement, a bullet crashed right into the car and landed in her handbag, which was on the floor between herself and her companion. It had cut her fountain pen in half but had injured no one.

Now followed six restful, delightful days in Nablus. There were changes there too—a great shortage of gasoline and fuel and the people were in fear of Jewish air raids, as Nablus was the capital of the central Arab districts. Foreign Arab armies were infiltrating the whole time, and the narrow valley between the mountains echoed from end to end with their gun practice and long volleys of shooting to celebrate the constant arrival of new troops and the news of any Arab successes. On my last day in Nablus there was great mourning for Sheikh Husseini, who had been killed while fighting in the Hebron district.

I was warned not to wander far away by myself, in case of being mistaken for a Jewess and being shot without previous questioning. Between Nablus and the little village of Rafidyah, where I had once lived, there was a hill with many olive trees and a flat terrace near the summit. It was high above the road, where I could be absolutely alone and undisturbed. Here, for four consecutive mornings I retired as soon as breakfast was over and spent long hours alone with the Lord.

It is impossible to describe what those quiet mornings did for me; it was as though I drank of a river of new life and was rested and strengthened. The whole terraced olive yard was thickly carpeted with tiny but brilliant flowers—white daisies, blue speedwell, pink flax, scarlet pheasant's eye, and cream scabious—while the cicadas chirped among the olives. Below the hill all the valley was green, and on the other side the steep quarry-scarred sides of Mount Ebal towered up to the sky like a red and yellow wall, while the outermost houses of Nablus were just visible. Goats and a few cows grazed on the hillside and occasionally came my way, their clanging bells the only sound to break the stillness.

I always began these quiet times of waiting on the Lord by echoing Solomon's prayer, "Give unto thy servant a hearing heart." So much seemed to depend upon being able to hear his voice and learn his plans. I dared not choose a single step for myself. He alone knew what lay ahead, and it was vital to learn his plan. During those four quiet days I began to understand what his will was for me. I had felt all along that he wanted me to remain in the country after the mandate ended, but was it to be in the Arab or Jewish area? Where did he want me to live, and what did he want me to do?

Gradually but quite clearly I came to understand that my place was to be among the Jewish people in that part of Jerusalem that would so soon be completely besieged and cut off from all the rest of Jewish Palestine. When I wondered why, I was shown the need of witnesses to remain among the Jewish people in their hour of trial. Over and over again I found him turning me to those wonderful verses in Ezekiel, about the valley of dry bones, and the miracle that happened to them. "And he said unto me, 'Son of man, can these bones live?' And I answered, 'O Lord GOD, thou knowest.' . . . Then he said unto me, 'Son of man, these bones are the whole house of Israel'" (Ezek. 37:3, 11).

As I pondered these and the following verses, I began to realize that the time of their fulfillment was arriving. All normal and accustomed mission work was coming to an end, but witnesses were still needed who would live among the

Jewish people. The dry bones of Israel were to experience two phases. The first would be a coming together in union as a nation, bound together with flesh and sinews. Then the second stage must certainly follow: a quickening into spiritual life and power.

"There was a noise, and behold a shaking, and the bones came together, bone to his bone . . . but there was no breath in them. Then said he unto me, 'Prophesy unto the wind, prophesy, son of man, and say to the wind, . . . "Come from the four winds, O breath, and breathe upon these slain, that they may live."' So I prophesied as he commanded me, and the breath came into them, and they lived, and stood up upon their feet, an exceeding great army" (Ezek. 37:7–10).

Morning after morning I pondered these verses and prayed for an understanding heart and found myself asking, *Is this really his word to me? his promise? Have we really reached this stage? Are we actually so honored as to be his witnesses among Israel in these last weeks or months or years that are to see their revival? Are we the intercessors who are to pray to the wind of heaven, "Come, O breath and breathe upon these slain that they may live?"*

At that time I am sure very few non-Jews thought that Israel would be able to stand against the invading armies and drive them out of the land. I myself did not expect that the Jewish state would so soon come into being and achieve success. I supposed that the Jewish people, while still in unbelief, would be unable in their own strength to bring to pass such a miracle. It was this expectation that made the thought of staying in the Jewish area while the Arabs achieved success such a nightmare, but by the end of those few days I was sure that God meant me to remain, so wonderful, glorious, and certain did the word seem as he spoke it, day by day, on that quiet hillside that at the time nothing seemed impossible. I felt neither fear nor shrinking, only an awed wonder and joy in the thought of being privileged to remain with others in the valley of dry bones and, at such a time, to pray for the breath of life to come to them.

But it was all very different when I came down from the mountaintop and looked at things from the earthly angle again. Even before I left Nablus we heard that the mandatory government was going to broadcast to the British community, urging all Britishers to leave Palestine before the end of the mandate and undertaking to provide facilities for their departure. At first, several hundred British civilians and businessmen had expected to remain in Jerusalem. But, already it was widely believed among the Jewish people that once the mandate was given up, Britain meant to support the Arab cause. In that case, all Britons would be enemies, and surely the Jewish authorities would not tolerate any of them remaining in the Jewish area.

What was the good of imagining that God was telling me to stay in Jewish Jerusalem if the Jews themselves would never permit it? And then I was constantly tormented by my imagination, picturing all the horrors that lay ahead: the siege, the breaking through of the Arab armies, the capture of the Jewish area, and the wiping out of the inhabitants. It would mean, I supposed, being cut off from all communication with the outside world, separated from friends and fellow missionaries, under constant fire, suspected by the Jews, and perhaps imprisoned, unable to get out even if I wanted to, I who so loved open spaces and being alone with freedom to move about.

The more I thought about these things, the more impossible it seemed. Perhaps God was only testing me to see if I was ready to do his will, and after I submitted to his guiding, he would lead me to remain in the Arab area, perhaps at the mission station in the Old City with the rest of the staff.

There we would not be besieged and would have a back door open in Transjordan.

But there, written down plainly in the little book I use in my quiet times, was the message I felt so sure he had given me during those mornings when I went alone to meet him, asking to be shown his will. Had it all been a mistake? Or was it really the word of the Lord? Anyhow I knew that the horrible pictures I was tempted to see in imagination were in all probability attempts by the enemy to get me out of the line of the Lord's will, just as he had so often done in the past. "Better hath he been for years, Than thy fears" were the words that came to my mind, as they had so often done before, bringing me great comfort.

On April 10 I returned to Jerusalem. As I drew near the outskirts of the city, following a number of other vehicles, I found the road lined with terror-stricken Arab women running along beside the cars and begging to know if the Jews were coming to attack their village. Then I heard the dreadful news that during the night a band of Jewish terrorists had raided the nearby village of Deir Yassin. They had killed all the men and burned the village, and now the women and children were being carried into Jerusalem and sent to the Old City for refuge.

As I drove up to the mission compound, just inside Jaffa Gate, British soldiers were even then bringing truckloads of these women, weeping and wailing for their murdered husbands and sons and lost homes, as they drove through the streets. The whole world was shocked by this massacre. But it should be remembered that Deir Yassin was one of the very first villages to fire on the Jewish suburbs and that the consistent sniping across the valley at Beit Hakerem had, for months, been causing death and homelessness to many Jews.

It was terribly difficult during these months to free one's mind from bitterness and the all-prevailing atmosphere of hate. Things were happening on all sides that shocked one to the heart, and one must remember that all reports from both sides were inclined to be distorted or at least to leave out extenuating circumstances or the reasons that led to such actions. And one needs to remember, too, that the names *terrorist* and *patriot* may be applied to the very same persons, depending entirely upon one's own point of view. Undoubtedly there were many on both sides who carried out these dreadful acts of violence who were heroic and sincere patriots, longing to liberate their people from foreign interference and gain possession of Palestine for their own people, Arabs or Jews as the case may be. But the frightful thing about any victory achieved by violence and force is the legacy of hate that it leaves behind and the seeds sown for further unleashing of strife and bloodshed.

When I got back after those days of holiday in Nablus, I found that plans were well under way for helping the Hebrew Christians leave the country. It looked as though no missionaries would be left in the Jewish area at all and, if they did stay, there would be no Hebrew Christian congregation left for them to minister to. The food situation was becoming dreadful. It seemed unlikely that rations would be spared to anyone but Jews, and that no one would be allowed to remain unless they were willing to help the war effort. Deep down in my heart I heaved a sigh of relief. It seemed that not only would I not be expected to stay in the Jewish area, but I would not be allowed to do so. As I tried to push on one side what the Lord had said on the hillside at Nablus, deep down in the innermost recess of my being, my will cried out longingly, *Don't let me miss thy will, Lord. Thou knowest that I trust thee to make and keep me willing.*

One day after lunch we had coffee in the sunny courtyard. As I went upstairs to my room, I was thinking with a half guilty satisfaction that after all I would be able to remain there at the mission house and be near the food market. Perhaps I would still be free to drive around, and if worse came to worst, I could retire to Transjordan. Suddenly an agonizing unrest seized me, the most dreadful mental disquiet. I remembered my Lord's words at Nablus and his call to live among the Jews as a witness. He had offered me the honor of being one of his watchmen, and here I was trying to evade and wriggle out of it. I said to myself again, *But we can't any of us live in the Jewish area. The authorities won't allow it.* Then in a dreadful flash I remembered Gideon's fleece, and the sign that God gave him that he was in God's will and not imagining his call. The Lord seemed to say, "If the authorities will give you permission to remain, are you willing to do so? That will be your fleece. Ruth told you yesterday that if it were possible she, too, would choose to stay in the Jewish area and try to carry on the girls' school. If the permission is granted, will you take it that that is what I want you both to do?"

The inner struggle became so unbearable that I went up on the rooftop alone, and the enemy pressed sore against me in what seemed an overwhelming attack. I felt an agony of dread and pain and horror. I couldn't do this thing. I couldn't voluntarily go and live in a besieged area, with who knew what horrors ahead and no way of escape. For a little while it was all pain, but thank God not a moment of rebellion. While my flesh cried out that I couldn't do it, my heart said, "I delight to do thy will, O my God."

And, amazingly impossible as it had looked, so it was arranged. But God, in his loving-kindness and gentleness, made it as easy as possible, for he did not ask me to stay alone but gave me the best of companions. A few days later we were told that three of us were to be allowed to live at the doctor's house on the hospital compound in the Jewish area: Ronald, one of the mission clergymen; Ruth, the head of the girls' school; and myself, to be the cook-housekeeper. The other two members of the mission were to stay and look after the mission church and compound in the Old City.[4] This was already filled with Arab-Christian refugees, and by the time we moved to the Jewish area, there were about fifty Arab and three or four British friends living there on the compound. It was lovely indeed that the mission could help, in this way, Christians in both areas.

A few days after this plan was settled, I went to spend the afternoon with Lilly, who was living in the American Church Compound near the hospital. It was one of our Friday prayer afternoons together, which we tried never to miss. She was a Hebrew Christian and told me that one of the leading missionaries had just been round to tell her that he had been warned again that all Hebrew Christians would have to leave the Jewish area. Even if they tried to remain, they would not be granted rations and would be treated as suspects. He had urged her to leave while the way was still open for escape.

This was indeed a dreadful blow. If Lilly, my special friend and prayer partner, left, I would indeed be bereft. *Must I really remain shut up in this dreadful Jewish area without her?* (For Ruth and Ronald were new, untried friends, and I didn't realize at this stage with what wonderful companions my Lord had put me.) I felt no one could take her place and could not help shedding some very bitter tears when she gave me this news, for she had felt as strongly as I did that the Lord was asking her to remain.

Lilly herself was in great conflict about the whole matter. She still believed in spite of this warning that the Lord meant her to remain as a witness, unless he made it utterly clear in some way that she had mistaken his call. His message to her had been so very clear that she did not think that she ought to allow any human warning to frighten her into disobedience.

She said to me, "God has been speaking to me so much through Psalm 118, and especially this promise in verse 17, when I shrank from possible danger, for I do feel afraid, 'I shall not die, but live, and declare the works of the LORD.' And he keeps turning me again and again to verse 27: 'Bind the sacrifice with cords, even unto the horns of the altar.' The Hebrew says 'thick cords,' so that there is no possibility for the sacrifice to escape."

Then she added simply, "I have offered the Lord my burnt sacrifice, and now that the fire begins to burn, shall I take it back?" It was like a knife in my heart. I longed to untie the cords now that the fire had begun and to take back the sacrifice. We sat there in her room, battling together against the enemy's assault, and then we prayed. We were like frightened little children, clinging to the Lord and claiming his clear guidance and his power to do his will even though we felt we couldn't.

It is true, his sheep do know his voice. We can safely trust him to lead us and not let us make a mistake, if we really want to do his will. We came to understand and later to experience that even in the midst of besieged Jerusalem he could "feed us in green pastures, and lead us forth beside the waters of comfort." As Bunyan tells us, "Our Lord is of very tender compassions to them that are afraid." And also to such as suffer from very vivid imaginations. He knows just how to help all his children.

Mrs. Gibson, one of two American missionaries who remained in Jewish Jerusalem, and with whom Lilly had gone to live, told us long afterwards that when she heard what a comforting promise God had given to us both, that we should not die but live, she had asked him to give her a reassuring word also about his safekeeping. Opening her Bible afterwards, the first words her eyes lighted on were, "Precious in the sight of the LORD is the death of his saints" (Ps. 116:15).

"I knew then," she said, "that I mustn't insist on being kept safe, but be ready for death, too, if by that means I might be his witness and fulfill his will." So according as he sees we are able to bear it, so he gives us his personal word and strengthens us to follow him.

6 *The End of the Mandate*

The last two weeks of April were sad and sorrowful; life was so busy, yet at the same time so entirely abnormal that everything that happened seemed quite unreal.

On April 13 the most horrible tragedy of all happened. One of the convoys going out to the Hadassah Hospital on Mount Scopus, contrary to existing regulations, had no military escort and was attacked by Arab forces. The convoy had received no permission for its journey from the British military authorities, nor was it escorted by them. Under the circumstances, the enemy forces apparently concluded that it was rightful prey.

For seven hours the vehicles of the convoy were stranded on the road, exposed to intermittent fire. A British military escort was sent to bring them back to Jerusalem as it was an unauthorized convoy, but they refused to return.

At the end of seven hours the Arab forces closed in on the convoy and massacred seventy-six persons, while twenty-one others were injured. Many of the victims were well-known doctors, the head doctor of the Hadassah Hospital being one of them, while others were professors at the Hebrew University. The Jewish people were aghast and furious that the British should have left them to such a fate. The military, on the other hand, rightly affirmed that they could not undertake to protect unauthorized convoys, which went at their own risk and in defiance of the emergency regulations.

On April 20 all members of the British community were summoned to a meeting in the German colony and were urged to leave the country before the expiry of the mandate, as war was inevitable and there were no means of guaranteeing their protection if they remained. At this stage, therefore, practically the whole British community decided to leave Jerusalem. A mere handful elected to remain in their homes in the German colony, trusting that things might settle down quickly once the mandate ended. Others decided to take shelter at St. George's Cathedral Close, in the Arab area near the future British consulate; and four or five others at Christ Church, inside the Old City; while we three missionaries elected to remain in the Jewish area and were the only British Christians who were able to do so.

April 25 was the first day of the Jewish Passover. A terrible battle raged all that night, and we lay cowering in our beds in the hostel, just inside the Jaffa Gate. The sky was red with flares and flashes, and the sound of crashing shells was nearly deafening. As usual, Yemen Moshe bore the brunt of the battle as did the Jewish quarter in the Old City.

News now came through from other parts of the country that during the past few days the Jews had taken possession of Tiberias in the north. On April 21 they got Haifa, the chief port of Palestine, except for the areas still occupied by the British army. A mass evacuation of Arabs was taking place. Hundreds of thousands were fleeing from their homes, and the beginning of the appalling Arab refugee problem was in full development. A few days later the Jewish Hagana stormed and took Acre and all the main part of Galilee, and nearly all the chief towns were in the hands of the Jews. Only the central triangle and the far south remained in Arab hands.

On April 25 Miss Andersson, a well-known and much-loved Swedish missionary, was killed by snipers as she was returning to her home on the Mount of Olives. There were of course no buses, and she was walking alone from Jerusalem to her home across the valley. For a long time she had been suspected of carrying parcels of food to her Jewish friends, and many had warned her not to risk her life in this way. But she was a true and faithful friend of both Jews and Arabs, and she could not bear to think that any of her friends must go short if she had it in her power to relieve their need.

On April 26 Lydda Airport was seized by the Jews. All of the main roads were now cut. Jerusalem was completely cut off at this stage from the rest of the country, and no convoys could get through. The same day, the postal services of the country came to an end, and for the time being, Palestine was isolated from the rest of the world. During the next three months there was no postal communication with Great Britain. On this same day, Mr. Denham was shot dead while leaving Barclay's Bank, and the following day Mr. Legett, the British consul in Haifa who was on a visit to Jerusalem, was killed.

On April 28 the last British civilians, except the little group who elected to remain, left Jerusalem in a military-protected convoy. On this day, too, King Abdullah of Trans-jordan declared war on the Jews. But on April 30 both Jews and Arabs agreed to a truce in the Old City.

It was the earnest desire of the retiring high commissioner, Sir Alan Cunningham, that before he left Jerusalem there should be a permanent truce and that both sides would allow the Holy City to remain neutral, while the Jewish and Arab armies fought, if fight they must, elsewhere. For a week or two we had high hopes that Sir Alan's earnest efforts would be rewarded and Jerusalem would be isolated from the war. But he was not permitted to carry out this last benefit to the country. He represented a regime too much hated to be allowed to retire with such a victory to his credit. Jerusalem, when he left, was to become the center of the maelstrom. So April ended and only two weeks remained before the laying down of the mandate.

By the beginning of May things were getting so dangerous in the city and the fighting was so continuous, it was obvious that if I intended to live in the Jewish area I must leave the hostel and move to the hospital compound as soon as possible. Otherwise I might very easily find myself stranded in the Arab area for the duration. No one knew how much longer the military zone would remain, and once that went there would be no means of passing from one belligerent area to the other.

Accordingly, on May 3, twelve days before the mandate was due to end, I went to join Ruth and Ronald who were already living in the hospital compound. When the mandate ended, about twelve Protestant missionaries and a handful of baptized Christians remained in the Jewish area. Curiously enough, most of us lived in the same road, the Street of the Prophets. We had all been connected with different missions or else working independently, and some of us were scarcely acquainted with one another. We belonged to about ten different denominations and nearly as many different nationalities, and the way in which God welded us into one united band will be described later.

The hospital compound was at one end of the Street of the Prophets, and here, in one of the doctor's houses in the garden, Ronald, Ruth, and I made our home. The upper flat formed our living quarters, and in the downstairs flat Ruth, assisted by two or three Jewish teachers, still ran the girls' school with about forty girls attending.

A little further along the road was the American Alliance Church. There Mrs. Gibson and Lilly lived, and with them a retired missionary, a Hebrew Christian and his family, and a number of refugees to whom they had offered a home. At the further end of the street was a Hebrew Christian pastor and his wife, members of the Dutch Reformed Church. Elsewhere were two Finnish missionaries and a Hebrew Christian colleague running a children's home, a retired Swedish missionary, and a Swiss lady who was not attached to any mission.

Outside the Jewish area, in what had been the British security zone, but which the Jews had managed to take possession of the moment the mandate ended, holding it as a military occupied area, about fifteen British families remained, as well as six hundred Greeks and Armenians and a few Arab Christians.

As soon as the first truce occurred, all the British families except one left the city. The minister of the Scottish church of St. Andrew's gallantly remained to guard the church property and to continue the services. He probably had a harder time than anybody, as the church was right in the front line overlooking the Old City wall, and he was entirely alone.

In the notorious Deir Abu Tor quarter, old Mr. and Mrs. Shelley, both over eighty years of age, refused to leave their home and remained there absolutely cut off from everybody else, while the hill changed hands twice over. Later on, the Hagana removed them to safety in the Jewish zone.

A few of the missionaries also remained in the Arab area, some at Christ Church inside the Old City and some in St. George's Cathedral Close on the outskirts of the city. The latter place was near the borders of both Arab and Jewish areas and repeatedly came in for shells from both sides. Christ Church, just behind the ancient citadel, was wonderfully spared. For although many shells fell on the compound, no real damage occurred, though the Armenian quarter just beside it was heavily damaged and many people lost their lives.

As far as we knew, apart from the members of the consulate staff who lived at the consulate just outside the Damascus Gate, the only other British people who remained in Jerusalem were five employees of the Jerusalem Electric Company in the Jewish military occupied zone. They were arrested en masse, accused of espionage, and spent time in prison, until one after another they were acquitted and left the country.

As the anxious housekeeper of our family, I took with me to the besieged area the following farmyard: two black hens named Jemima and Keren-Happuch that, I hoped, would provide us with eggs; four pigeons that were to produce families and would from time to time afford us a change of diet from tinned foods; and a tiny yellow and white kitten named Mercy that was to keep rats and mice away from the premises. And of course there was Charles.

On May 3, therefore, the blue van "cackled and meowed" its way out of the Arab area and into the Jewish. Charles was bitterly resentful of the advent of Mercy and was openly relieved when the poor little thing proved too young to be able to subsist on tinned food and, after a distressing illness, came to an untimely death. The fowls and pigeons, however, more than fulfilled the duties expected of them. Although Jemima and Keren loudly protested at first, they quickly took to their new home and worked like two black angels, supplying us with nearly three hundred eggs in the ensuing seven months, at a time when the inhabitants of Jerusalem had practically forgotten what an egg looked like. Later on, Turkish eggs were occasionally obtainable in the shops. Sometimes these were all right, sometimes all wrong. Once I gingerly cracked one of the infrequent rations of Turkish eggs, and one after the other they exploded in my face like small, black bombs, making the kitchen almost unendurable. The pigeons produced family after family, a very welcome addition to our diet.

In spite of all of God's loving reassurances, I must confess that I moved to the Jewish area in a state of great depression and reluctance. Of course, we were all dead tired after the strain of these eventful and hectic weeks, and the first entries in my diary reflect this.

When reading other people's experiences, I never feel satisfied with a mere relation of events. I am always passionately curious to know just how the people really felt and how they reacted to unusual conditions. Particularly have I often tried to imagine the feelings of people in a besieged city, though never expecting to be in one myself.

So I have decided to copy the actual notes I jotted down day after day and let them present the scenes as I recorded them at the time. To some the personal element may appear unnecessary and irritating. To others, perhaps it will fill in the pictures and make them seem more real and human. And perhaps there are other Miss Much-afraids who will be comforted to read how wonderfully and with what special gentleness our heavenly Father undertook for a particularly fearful and shrinking soul.

It is pleasant to turn from the dreary remarks that I wrote during the first few days to the following entry, written on the last day of the mandate.

May 13

It has been an astonishingly happy ten days since I left the hostel and came to live in the Jewish area. The first three days were difficult; I was so tired, and the new life was so strange, and I felt so depressed at coming into this area. Cooking and washing up and housework are things that I have always hated, and there seemed so many extra jobs to catch up on that it was all overwhelming. And the cooking went wrong, which was most depressing. There is a great difference I find between acting as housekeeper to a large staff of servants and having to do every single thing oneself.

But now the strange fact is that I really enjoy it. Lilly has been kind, coming in and showing me how to do things and cooking some of the meals for me. And now I find even the cooking a real interest and pleasure and a wonderful relaxation after the strain of these past months. Also there has been a truce in Jerusalem for nearly a week, no shooting and no shells, and I can still drive to the Old City for groceries and vegetables. All three of us went down there for a service on Sunday. We are beginning to hope that, after all,

Jerusalem will be isolated from the fighting, and we shall be able to come and go freely.

It is a pleasure to look after the live creatures. I do love taking care of animals, even this fanatical and troublesome pair of pullets, Jemima and Keren-Happuch. For a week they were most grudging and obstinate and were always trying to escape, but now they have started laying eggs. I let them run about in the garden every afternoon, after the schoolgirls have gone home, and they scratch and enjoy themselves. The pigeons won't budge from their dark room, but both pairs have eggs.

I know I am strained and nervy, and I feel sorry for Ruth and Ronald. He is the essence of kindness and imperturbable good temper and not only acts as a furniture remover from morning to night, but is at everybody's beck and call and never shows a sign of irritation at any of the multitudinous calls made upon him. It makes me feel terribly ashamed and doubly thankful for my quiet, peaceful life in the kitchen.

Of course it would not be dear old difficult Jerusalem if there were not inconveniences to contend with. The electricity is cut for several hours every day, but it does come on sometimes. The water supply has been cut off from the Jewish area for a whole week, but we have our own good cistern water. And our telephone is still in order. The disposal of rubbish, now that the municipality no longer functions, is a major problem. For many weeks garbage has not been collected, and the streets are frightfully littered. We carry it here and there and burn what we can. We hopefully put two bins full of rubbish out in the road, as rumor had it the Jewish authorities were organizing garbage clearance. These bins were eventually emptied, but the bigger one was carried off.

There is no kerosene, Jerusalem's main fuel, and cooking for most people is a terrible problem, as they have no electricity either. Of course there never has been coal, and now there is neither wood nor charcoal coming in from the villages. We are very fortunate in this matter, as I was able to fetch a few tins of kerosene from the Second Company before it closed down. We are on the same line that supplies electricity to the hospital, so that when they have it, we have it too. Our drainage system keeps going wrong and the fouled water floods the garden, but one of our old workmen comes to see to it. We still have fresh vegetables and fruit, which I fetch from the Old City, though there has been none in the Jewish shops for nearly six months. All the posts closed over a week ago, so we are completely cut off from the rest of the world, and in two days' time the mandate ends.

But in spite of this formidable list of difficulties, we manage wonderfully and keep in excellent health. The garden is so pleasant, and there are trees everywhere. Our storeroom is stocked, and we receive very much kindness and help from the hospital authorities. There are over a hundred war casualties in the wards already. Lilly and Mrs. Gibson live nearly next door, so we have their friendship and fellowship to count on. Also, although it is May, the weather is still cool, and there are even showers to freshen things up. Our little home is like a sheltered oasis, where God in his marvelous goodness has given us a quiet resting place in the midst of a very stricken city.

May 14, 1948, 5:00 A.M.

The last day of the mandate. Last night at 9:30 on the radio, we heard the high commissioner make his farewell speech, a difficult one, but sensible and good, and with no sentimental nonsense about it. He ended abruptly with "good-bye." It was very depressing. It broke over me for the first time that Britain, our own nation, was leaving the Holy Land. And it was particularly depressing as heavy firing had just broken out around the Old City. The Jerusalem truce of the last few days seems over. They won't even let the High Commissioner leave with the comfort of feeling that the truce he strove so hard to arrange was succeeding.

This morning I woke at 4:30 and have just made my early morning cup of tea before electricity is cut at 5:00 A.M. The guns are firing heavily and continuously, and yesterday morning we were all so hopeful that Jerusalem would be isolated from the war and remain a Red Cross city. Today the British troops begin to leave. I hope the neutral zone will be open still, at least until Monday, as I have still things to buy for the little missionary group and for ourselves.

But how wonderfully God has helped us. Tonight the mandate ends. But our house is all in order, and we face the future with most of our frantic preparations ended. Everything is safely moved up here, including the livestock. The Arab refugees are installed at the mission house in the Old City, and our home was cleaned from top to bottom yesterday. We face whatever is coming with a clean house and clean bodies, as we all managed to get baths yesterday, and Ruth and I to wash our hair. What this means after the bustle and dust and dirt of these last few weeks, can only be felt, not described. So we turn to the future, and the new chapter that begins for Palestine tomorrow.

The *Daily Light* reminds us that here we have no continuing city and that we need to keep "looking unto Jesus, the author and finisher of our faith."

The *Palestine Post* of May 14 wrote in the following way of the events of this historic occasion:

Today is End-of-the-Mandate Day. By tonight no British official will be left in Jerusalem, and the last English news bulletin is due to be broadcast at lunchtime.

At 8 o'clock this morning the High Commissioner will leave Government House, which he entered for the first time on November 21st, 1945. After inspecting a guard of honor, Sir Alan will drive to Kalandia Airport, north of Jerusalem, and fly to Haifa, where he will be piped aboard the HMS Eurylus by a guard of honor. As he boards the ship a salvo of seventeen guns will be fired.

At midnight, the minute the mandate is over, the High Commissioner will sail for Britain.

At a last gathering with local and foreign correspondents yesterday, the Public Information Officer described briefly the program of the day. At 6.45 am the Union Jack will be lowered from the King David Hotel where the Government Administration Offices have been housed, to be replaced by the International Red Cross flag.

The moment Sir Alan's plane leaves Kalandia Airport, the British flag will be taken down from Government House, which is to be taken over by the Red Cross.

The Public Information Officer recalled that the British Government had always stated that it would lay down the mandate before May 15th. In keeping with its traditional punctuality, this was now being done.

All day yesterday British troops were busy in Zone B, where most of them have been stationed in recent weeks, collecting their kit, putting new tires on trucks and jeeps and armored cars, and getting ready to pull out at a moment's notice. Furniture was piled on the streets, kit bags were strewn along the pavements, and laundry was hurriedly shifted on the line with the moving sun, so that it would dry in time. Soldiers waved good-byes to passers-by, and there was much handshaking. Sergeant Majors and Subalterns were surrounded by clusters of soldiers, giving them last minute instructions.

Naturally we three British citizens, remaining almost as enemy aliens in the country, found this a strange time. We felt very grieved for the high commissioner, whom we had respected and admired as a man who honestly sought the good of the country. He had carried himself nobly and with great dignity in an increasingly impossible situation. His farewell speech that he broadcast to the country on May 13 was fine, and we felt as we listened that he had indeed done his very best. I append a part of it here:

> *Tomorrow at midnight the final page of the history of Palestine and the British Mandate in Palestine is turned. On the morrow a new chapter begins, and Palestine's history goes on.*
>
> *It is not my wish at this period of the British departure to turn back the pages and look at the past. It would be easy in doing so to say some time, "there we did right," and no doubt at other times, "there we did wrong." In this complex matter of the Government of Palestine, the way ahead has not always been clear, and the future has often been obscured. In this respect we are more than content to accept the judgment of history.*
>
> *Rather would I wish to say only, if it shall be that by our going we bring eventual good to the peoples of Palestine, none of us will cavil at our departure.*

I do not believe that the endeavors to find agreement between the Jews and Arabs did not bear seed. In all our efforts we have failed to find soil in which it could germinate. Equally, I am convinced that the solution of this problem is not to be reached by bullets or bombs, which have never brought a solution to any problem, but only misery. To those of us who have lived here during the past thirty years, this fact is only too evident.

And therefore, even at this late hour, I pray that peace may come immediately to Palestine, peace emanating from the hearts of the peoples themselves, the only true instrument by which it can be achieved, a peace built on enduring foundations, on conciliation and in friendship, made lasting in unselfishness, and perhaps sacrifice. For it is clear that both Arab and Jew, each in his own sphere, can contribute much to the other's welfare.

Even if this unhappy conflict must come, there is yet time to isolate the Holy City from it, and continuing efforts to this end have been made. A "cease-fire" has now been achieved in Jerusalem, and I make here my most earnest and final recommendation to both Jews and Arabs that it shall be sustained, strengthened, and extended.

We who are leaving here have experienced great sadness in the past years, a sadness that much could have been accomplished and had to be left undone. Friendship and goodwill were marred by events. But in our memories will live many happy associations with Palestine, and in our hearts will remain the constant desire that cooperation, goodwill and amity may be re-established between us, to our mutual benefit in the future. Good-bye.

Part 2

A New Chapter Begins: The State of Israel

"There was a noise, and behold a shaking, and the bones came together, bone to his bone. And when I beheld, lo, the sinews and the flesh came upon them, and the skin covered them above: but there was no breath in them" (Ezek. 37:7–8).

7 *The Siege of Jerusalem*

he State of Israel is born. The first independent state in nineteen centuries was born in Tel-Aviv, as the British Mandate over Palestine came to an end at midnight on Friday, and it was immediately subjected to the test of fire. As Medinat Yisrael (State of Israel) was proclaimed, the battle for Jerusalem raged, with most of the city falling to the Jews. A few hours later, Palestine was invaded by Moslem armies from the south, east and north, and Tel-Aviv was raided from the air. Between Thursday night and this morning, Palestine went through what, by all standards, must be among the most crowded hours in its history (Palestine Post, *May 15, 1948*).

May 14

Well, the new chapter has opened, and the old chapter of the British Mandate in Palestine closed last night at midnight. And here we still are, a tiny group of missionaries left in Jerusalem at this momentous crisis. And what a day! The opening lines of the new chapter are not very pleasant.

I got up at 4:30 A.M. and just made tea before the electricity was turned off. At 7:30 A.M. Charles and I set off in the van to visit the Old City and to do some shopping before the zone closed. I meant to have breakfast at the mission hostel, and in the afternoon we were all to gather there for united prayer before being divided, perhaps for months. But when I reached the British barricade the soldiers told me that all zone passes would expire at 8:30 A.M., i.e., in half an hour's time. After that the zone would be unprotected, open to anyone; both Jews and Arabs were waiting to rush in and get possession of it first. This was a nasty shock indeed, and I hurried on to the mission house.

There were armed Arabs everywhere. Ramadan, our faithful hostel handyman, took one basket and went to the market. I took the other. Between us we managed to collect the most important things: fresh meat and vegetables. I got three tins of dry yeast so that I would be able to bake our bread, as we had no ration books. And then I just got back through the barricades at 8:20 A.M., and so home to the hospital compound to breakfast.

That was the last of all the nerve-racking trips of the previous six months. When I put the van away in the garage, I wondered just how long it would be before I could use it again, for there was no gasoline in the area, and none but essential vehicles were allowed on the roads. Everything was transported now on wheelbarrows or baby carriages or homemade and hand-pushed conveyances.

When I reached the hospital, the ambulances were already bringing in the Jewish dead and wounded from the Kfar Etz-Zion group of settlements in the Hebron District.

They surrendered last night after the Arab legion broke through their defenses. All of the Jewish men settlers were killed, even those who surrendered, and the largest of the settlements was burned to the ground. The radio said that the big Arab town of Jaffa had surrendered to the Jews and signed a treaty.

I spent the morning baking and cooking. At 10:00 A.M. spasmodic firing started. It got worse and went on all day. Our electricity was cut off by a bullet through the wire, so we could not hear the last English news bulletin at 1:30 P.M. But by 9:15 P.M. the hospital line was repaired, and we listened in to the one English broadcast the Jewish Hagana are to give each day. This is all we are left with. How queer it seems.

All British officials and all the military left Jerusalem today, and the Jews, quicker than the Arabs, have already managed to occupy most of the neutral zones. They have also taken Barclays Bank, right on the border of the Arab area, the main post office, and the huge Generali police building. There are no neutral zones left. So at present we are quite cut off from the rest of the mission. The evacuation of the zones so soon, and the laying down of the mandate one day early, came as a complete surprise.

As night fell and we were listening to the Hagana news bulletin in England, the firing became heavy, and all night long the guns rattled and crashed. Now as I write, very early in the morning of May 15, the firing is incessant and apparently nearer. Bullets keep whizzing past, but the heavy artillery is further away.

May 15

This is the second day of the new Jewish state. It is strange to sit here in my pleasant room, with its six sides and three windows, gaily striped Gaza rugs on the floor,

surrounded by plants and flowers and all my pictures, with
the trees by the windows full of blossom, while outside in the
darkness, battle is in full blast, with bullets whizzing and the
shooting incessant.

Things out here change so amazingly quickly. For weeks
we looked forward to months of siege and warfare. Then last
week there was a truce, and we began to think Jerusalem
would be proclaimed a Red Cross city and there would be
no more fighting. Now it is all changed again. The truce is
over, and the Jews seem to be taking the whole city.

The BBC news from London says the Egyptian army has
invaded the south, the Syrians are in the north, and Transjordan troops are already here—in and around Jerusalem.
Iraqi troops are on the way. Tel Aviv was bombed this
morning from the air. It all seems grotesquely as though history has flowed backwards thousands of years and all
Israel's old enemies of Bible times are gathered against her.
The names of the invading armies sound more like B.C. than
A.D. The news also said that the Jewish troops are storming
Acre and that America has already recognized the Jewish
state.

In the middle of the morning Ruth came to me carrying a
smoking bullet. It had crashed in through her window, just
missed the kitten, and burned a hole in the carpet. Thank
God she was not hit. It was not pleasant, but the Lord was
keeping us safe for a purpose.

Meanwhile sharp firing continued nearly all morning.
Rumor had it that the Jews had reached Jaffa Gate, but
later on we learned this was not so. We had no electricity
after 8:30 A.M., so we couldn't hear the news. There was also
a rumor that a truce had been signed in Jerusalem, but it
sounded very unlikely, as the fighting continued in full
swing.

It was a horrid afternoon. The fighting has been terribly close, the bullets hissing past all the time and lots of explosions. While I was resting in my room this afternoon, I was really frightened. The crashes were so near, with the bullets whining so close, and the thought that there is no longer a British army to intervene as in the past increased my fear. I was so frightened I slunk out of my room for a few moments. But God gave such an amazing sense that we were kept for a special work that I feel certain we shall not be harmed. I know this is selfish thinking when so many others are being wounded, but I am such a coward that I confess I do find it infinitely comforting. It is helpful, too, to have the cooking and baking to do. It keeps me busy and interested.

Now the firing is even worse. The bullets are rattling down, not just whizzing past. Maybe they are aiming at the police billet.

Now it is time to put the kettle on for tea. Sudden rapture! Disconsolately putting out my hand to test the lamp, I found the electricity was on again at long last, and rushing from the room I told the others and then plugged in the electric kettle, while Ronald hurried to the radio to try and get the London news. But alas, it is not time for a bulletin.

A few moments later a bullet violently ricocheted off a tree just outside the window and made us jump. The electricity remained on just long enough for us to boil a kettle and make some toast. Then it went off again for the rest of the evening, which meant no news on the radio.

During tea the Arabs started mortar shells. They fell quite near—a very different sensation from listening to Katamon and Yemen Moshe being shelled. This was us. It went on and got worse, and we went downstairs to shelter in the storeroom, which is the safest place.

Altogether not a nice beginning to a new chapter.

May 16, Whitsunday

There was a great deal of shooting all the night, but I was too tired to stay frightened and slept till 4:30 A.M., when to my joy I found the electricity was on and got up.

It was very pleasant waking in this large, bright room, the morning fresh and clear, birds singing blithely, the acacia tree in the police billet in full bloom. I can lie in bed and revel in its great clumps of white flowers. There was no firing, and so I had an uninterrupted quiet time with the Lord. How good he is to put me in this peaceful spot, when such a tempest is raging. Today is Whitsunday, and for the first time we cannot get to church. But we have access to him.

Evening

The second page of the new chapter has been even more unpleasant than the first. There has been constant shooting, and we hear that the Jews have taken all the zones and most of Jerusalem. But now the Arabs have started to shell from Nebi Samwil, the hill where Samuel is supposed to be buried. It towers high and overlooks the whole of Jerusalem. Ruth called me out of the kitchen for something, and while we were standing in the passage talking together, a shell fell on Cadbury ward and broke the roof, only a few yards from our house. Our kitchen window blew in, and a thousand pieces flew across the room. It was good there was no one in there.

At our tiny little Communion service (only the three of us were there) this first Sunday in the new Jewish state, Ronald read to us the words our Lord himself spoke here in Jerusalem so short a time before the Jewish state came to an end nineteen hundred years ago: "My peace I give unto you. . . . Let not your heart be troubled, neither let it be afraid" (John 14:27).

And at the little afternoon service when four of us gathered, it was the gift of love our Lord promised us. It seemed unspeakably wonderful, here in this battle-torn city, with shells raining down, to be able to sing those beautiful words:

From the overshadowing
Of Thy gold and silver wing,
Shed on us who to Thee sing,
Holy, heavenly Love.

Tonight all the clocks in the Jewish area of Jerusalem are to be put forward two hours, so as to save daylight. It will be light till 8:30 P.M., and we won't need lamps. But the Arab area is keeping to the old time.

May 17

Here we are starting our fourth day of war. It begins with heavy firing and heavy explosions. The electrician has mended the line that was cut when a shell fell on Cadbury ward, and Ruth and Ronald listened in to the BBC from London, which reported that a terrible battle had been raging in Jerusalem. Twenty Britons had gathered at the cathedral service in the Arab area on Whitsunday, but the noise was so great they could hardly hear the service. It also reported that a battle was raging for the Jewish part of the Old City, and that the Jews there were expected to surrender during the night.

Evening

What a day! The new chapter gets worse and worse. We began the day with double summer time, painfully rising two hours earlier, while the Arab side still slumbered. At lunch Ronald told us that our British consul in the Arab area had been allowed to ring up to ask how we were, the bishop having told him about us. The bishop's line was cut, but it was very cheering to hear from the consul. Somehow we didn't realize he was there, and it seemed strange to think of all the British troops away and this dreadful war raging.

Firing and explosions continued all day, but after tea the Arabs began terrible heavy shelling of the whole Jewish area from all sides. Shells crashed all around us, some of them fearfully near. They kept on till darkness fell, and we ate a cold supper, sheltering in the central room we have made into a chapel. Ambulances were running in and out of the hospital compound all the time.

Lilly came to see us today. It was brave of her to venture out. She said yesterday a bullet came in through the roof of her room and embedded itself in the wall behind her bed, just where her head would have been if she had been resting as usual. But she was late with her work and had stayed in the kitchen washing dirty pans. Within four days of the end of the mandate we have all had narrow escapes. How wonderful God is.

The BBC reporters shut up at St. George's reported to England that the fighting today had not been so bad. We all exclaimed when we heard this on the radio. It depends what area one is in. The shelling in our part has been worse than anything before.

May 18

A shocking night, the worst I have ever known. Battle raged all night long, all over Jerusalem. Thirty-two Jews were killed, and we don't know how many Arabs, and we heard later that several people in the crowded Armenian quarter next to Christ Church had been killed. We also heard that Archdeacon MacInnes was shot in the leg, and is now in the French Hospital just outside the New Gate where some of the worst fighting is going on. Also, another man was shot and wounded on the roof of the British consulate.

Our two hens remain undisturbed by the falling shrapnel, though it litters the garden. They continue to lay one or two eggs every day. The eggs I stored in salt three months ago are still keeping well.

May 19th

By far the worst night so far. The shelling was really appalling. At 1:30 A.M. Ruth came to my room and called me. Ronald was up too. We went down to the chapel and had a prayer for stricken Jerusalem and especially for our friends in the Old City, as it seemed to be the center of attack. About 2:30 A.M. it quieted a bit, and we went upstairs. Ronald made us Ovaltine, and we listened to the news from America, which said the Arab legion was attacking the Jewish quarter in the Old City. Then to bed again about 3:00 A.M., but it got so bad that Ruth and I dressed and went down to the chapel. I took some pillows and a blanket and lay down on some pew cushions on one of the benches and actually slept till about 7:00 A.M. After breakfast three teachers came, but no children. The teachers brought a one-page *Palestine Post*. It said the Jews had captured Bishop Gobat school on Mount Zion, from which the Arabs had been shelling the Jewish quarter.

Just before washing up the luncheon things, I went to let Jemima and Keren run loose in the garden and to collect the daily egg. As I was stooping to unlock the gate, there was a colossal explosion just behind. Splinters of shrapnel and bits of tree fell all around, but nothing touched me. I raced indoors and found Ruth, white as a sheet, thinking I had been blown to bits.

We found the shell had fallen on the roof of Norfolk ward, just beside our house. The veranda roof was smashed, the electric cable cut, three holes made in the main roof, and tiles littered everywhere. A lot more of our windows had been blown in, and a splinter of shrapnel had cut off the leg of a desk in the schoolroom. We were deeply thankful that none of the patients in the ward was hurt and for our own escape. Only a few yards nearer and the shell would have demolished the garage and the precious van.

Several more shells fell near us, and at 1:00 P.M. the front of the American Church was badly hit. Later we heard that the nice old Christian man who did the church's odd jobs had been hit just outside the gate of their compound. He was brought to our hospital and died almost at once due to loss of blood.

We were kept busy cleaning up the kitchen, taking shelter every few minutes, and then sweeping up more glass and removing fragments.

Ronald got the supper. He is very handy about the house and does this once a week to give me a free evening. The shelling was so heavy we decided to move a stove and pans and crockery down to the storeroom, so that we can cook downstairs if this heavy shelling continues.

I used to try and imagine what things would be like when the British left and real war began. Well it is all happening as I imagined. But what I didn't foresee, though I ought to have done so, was all the joy and peace the Lord gives and the continual sense of his presence and help. Nor did I foresee how much I would prefer to be in the Jewish side of the city, nor the pleasure I got in the cooking and housework. Everything that goes on seems intensely interesting, and life is overflowingly full. Our home is a little heavenly oasis in the midst of the valley of the shadow of death. The streets are deadly, dangerous places, the hospital just next door reeks of death, and the mountains round about Jerusalem are full of armies and gun emplacements. But inside our green fences there is something I cannot describe, but which makes me worship and rejoice and fills me with steady happiness. I think Dr. Moffatt's translation of Philippians 3:20 best describes it: "Ye are a colony of heaven."

May 20

The big Hadassah Hospital and the Hebrew University on Mount Scopus were evacuated and rumors were widespread. The Jews in the Old City surrendered today. It is now in flames. Last night was comparatively quiet, although there were sporadic crashes. I did not have to leave my bed, though I could not sleep. At 6:30 A.M. a continual stream of shells began swishing overhead and then crashing down. Last night's news bulletin said that the Arab legion had retaken the police billet on Mount Scopus, which dominates Jerusalem.

It is just one week today since the mandate was given up.

May 24

We have had some times of terrible shelling and some very narrow escapes, but the Lord continues to undertake for us in a marvelous way. The American consul-general, Mr. Wasson, was shot on Saturday and was brought to this hospital, where he died. His body now lies in our house, waiting for burial, as the hospital outbuildings are already overcrowded with bodies, sixty or more waiting for Jewish burial, and he, of course, is a Christian. Ronald is to conduct his funeral. It is terribly difficult getting people buried, as all the cemeteries are outside the city and cut off by Arab armies. Another member of the American consulate has also died of wounds and lies in the ward next door.

We heard on the radio that three shells fell on St. George's Close. One went through the nave of the cathedral, one exploded in a bedroom, and one fell on the garage and wrecked the bishop's car.

Meanwhile the Egyptian army is stationed at Bethlehem and has reached the outskirts of Jerusalem, after destroying the nearby Jewish settlement of Ramat Rachel. The Iraqi and Syrian armies are devastating the north. It sounds grotesquely as though we were hearing the news bulletins of millenniums past. The Arab legion (not the Roman legions this time) has overcome the Jewish quarter in the Old City and set it on fire. They are burning it synagogue by synagogue. The inhabitants surrendered after holding out till all their ammunition was gone. The Red Cross supervised the evacuation, and we were told that the Arab legion treated the women, children, and old people with every consideration.

We have not been outside the compound for days. All the shops are shut, and no food convoys can get through. For a long time before this, the shops had nothing on their shelves but tea and baking powder. The latter was of no use to anyone as there is no flour to be bought. But there is so much I want to thank the Lord for. He has helped so wonderfully, in so many ways. I never could have imagined how lovely he would be.

May 26

There was heavy shelling all over the Jewish area, and at 3:00 A.M. airplanes came over. Ruth and I went downstairs. The Khamsin (east wind) was frightful, and we ache with tiredness, but praise God for safety.

Aili[5] came in just before lunch. She had only ventured out into the open streets because she heard that Ammi, one of her adopted boys, was seriously wounded at Ramat Rachel, the settlement that the Arabs have succeeded in razing to the ground. He is still only sixteen years old, but was sent to help at the settlement while the older men fought. He was horribly wounded and had to crawl about in agony till he was found.

The Swedish school is reported to be on fire. It is right in no-man's-land, and both sides fight to get possession of it. Fortunately our Swedish friends left weeks ago.

The doctor on night duty at the Red Shield (Jewish Red Cross) next door sleeps on a stretcher in our hall, as there is no quiet place over there where he can lie down when he comes off duty. He told us that on Wednesday, from 7:00 P.M. till 1:00 A.M., a continual stream of casualties came in. When he came off duty at 1:00 A.M., the heaviest shelling was only just beginning. That night was the worst so far. Of course, we all slept downstairs. Airplanes passed overhead nine times. We thought they were Arab, but they turned out to be Jewish.

Later in the morning while I was cooking, seven or eight shells crashed down, seemingly on top of us. As I sped downstairs I saw a sheet of fire between our house and the garden wall where the garage is, then flames and stifling smoke. It looked certain that a shell had hit the garage and set fire to the precious van. The schoolgirls were huddled in the hall, and though the big schoolroom faces that direction, no one was hurt. As the smoke cleared away we saw that the fire was a few feet in front of the garage, where an incendiary bomb had fallen beside the door. I rushed out and threw earth on the hole and damped down the flame, and presently the dry grass burned out, and no damage was done.

That night the radio said that King Abdullah of Transjordan was in Jerusalem, and he had prayed for victory in the Dome of the Rock. Fires are still raging in the Old City, and the great synagogue is on fire.

May 28

Thank God for a quiet night, the first for a long time. I slept on a little bed down in the chapel. Ruth sleeps in the office downstairs, and Ronald's room is on the ground floor anyway. Lilly sleeps in the basement of the American Church, with about fifty other people who have no shelter in their homes.

Hard and terrible things have happened since I wrote only four days ago. Every day seems to get worse, and yet the Lord gives such joy and peace. We keep in excellent health, and there is always plenty to occupy us, though Ruth and I never leave the compound. Ronald wanders about everywhere helping people. When he is outside we cringe when the shells fall near, in case he won't come back. So many, many people have been killed.

There has been a scorching east wind all this week, and this makes things harder. One cannot sleep or relax for a moment, and it drains one of strength. Shells explode continuously. I don't even cross the garden to the chicken run without lifting my heart in prayer for safety.

About 10:00 A.M. this morning there were two or three terrible explosions, and we saw that a shell had just cleared our back garden wall and the garage and burst on a car in front of the police billet. In a moment or two the car was burned out. Later in the day the public works building was on fire. Rumor also says an incendiary bomb hit the Egged bus station, and their precious gasoline caught fire.

The radio reports that day and night the Arabs continue to burn the Jewish quarter of the Old City, and they have burned the great Hurva Synagogue. Thousands of Jews and Arabs are still fighting a major battle in the Babil Wad area and round Latrun, with the Jews struggling to open the road for food convoys to Jerusalem and the Arabs trying to keep it closed. The Latrun water pumping station that supplies Jerusalem is in Arab hands, and not a drop of water can come through.

Now it is evening. I am sitting on the terrace and dodging into the chapel when I hear shells starting out on their deadly journey. I have just been to visit Aili's wounded boy, Ammi. He is in this hospital. Two kind nurses let me in, though it was after visiting hours, to what used to be our bright, airy, peaceful Chaplin ward. What a scene. It was packed with beds, like sardines in a tin, the light shut out, stifling hot, and every bed with a terribly wounded man on it. A room burdened with pain. Ammi lay near the door. He is only sixteen years old, and he has lost an eye and part of his face has been blown away.

That terribly grim room and all other wards are dreadful to think about. So many are lying in the hospitals in this stifling Khamsin, fighting the heat, with thirst adding to the sufferings of their wounds.

Perhaps I may add here, that after that first visit to Ammi, I often used to go over to the wards with jugs of icy water from our Frigidaire and go round from bed to bed, giving water to those who were parched with fever. At that time the wards were so crowded that the hospital had difficulty in supplying enough cold, boiled water to meet the need. It was a very small thing to do but was the one way in which I could help. Long afterwards, complete strangers would accost me in the streets like old friends. When I was obliged to admit that I didn't recognize them, they would remind me of those cups of iced water in the wards, when they were so bandaged one could not see their faces or so suffering even their friends could hardly recognize them. Ronald was splendid over visiting in the wards and carrying cheer and help. Several monks were wounded at various times, as well as members of the Red Cross and U.N. staff, and they all came to this hospital.

June 6

For the first time in what seems ages, I am actually sitting on our garden veranda, listening for the shells that make me dive indoors. It is not quite a month since the British gave up the mandate, and many weeks since any convoys got through to Jerusalem with supplies. We are besieged with armies of all the neighboring countries around Jerusalem. There is, at least, a beginning of famine, with the ration of 150 grams of bread each day for each person and hardly anything else. Those who did not, or could not, lay in stores are beginning to starve. Lilly and Mrs. Gibson know of many pitiful cases of elderly or sick people who will not beg or ask for help. They literally live on dry bread and water, as they cannot even boil a kettle for tea.

The shelling has gone on intermittently for almost four weeks now and is a great trial. Sometimes whole families have been wiped out by one explosion, though generally it is only people in the open streets who get killed. Yesterday was our worst day, and shells and incendiaries fell all over the hospital compound.

In the last two weeks over a thousand casualties have been treated in this hospital alone. Ammi has been moved to another temporary hospital at San Joseph, the Roman Catholic girls' school, a little further along the road. They move patients there as soon as they are out of danger, as the beds here are all needed for the new cases. Happily Ammi is making good progress. I went to visit him at San Joseph. He and the other patients were lying in the cellars out of the way of the shells. It is really magnificent to see how the Hadassah is coping with this terrible emergency. But the lack of space and the numbers to be dealt with make it terribly difficult.

Down there in the cellars it was like a scene from the experiences of Florence Nightingale in the Crimea: the long, narrow cellar with arches, so that one looked down the whole length of it, gratings near the ceiling to let in light and air; and bodies with every conceivable kind of wound. Most of them lay on narrow beds nearly touching one another, but some only had mattresses on the floor. The boy in the bed next to Ammi had lost both hands and probably the sight of both eyes, though there is just a chance one eye may partially recover. Two elderly men sat beside him, and the girl, still in her teens, to whom he was engaged, waved away flies during the precious hour in which visitors were admitted. What a price in sacrifice and maimed young lives the Jewish state has had to pay.

On Saturday night we could hardly close our eyes all night long. We were all quietly busy when the worst outbreak of all began. Ruth was dusting and sweeping the chapel ready for the Sunday services, while Ronald was repainting the red crosses on our gate and ducking in every now and then when he heard the shells coming. I was busy in the pigeon room, fixing a netted door to give more light.

Then the shells got in our range again, and there was pandemonium. We went to bed in the storeroom. The electric cable was cut, and we were all plunged into darkness with the shells crashing down. From one to three in the morning was the worst time. I lay cowering, with my stomach turning over, but it was not mental fear, only physical reaction to the awful crashes, each one feeling as though it would smash us to pieces.

At 3:15 A.M., it quieted down somewhat and Mr. Datzi arrived at Ronald's window. He said that his wife had had one of her bad heart attacks, and could he and Ruth go across to their house. They went at once, and Ruth sat with her till morning, though she was quite unconscious.

At 9:00 A.M. we had Communion, just the three of us. The shells were still crashing down, but so far we had had no experience of damage from a direct hit, so we carried on. The shelling continued all day, but was followed by the quietest night so far.

June 7

One queer thing I did not foresee, nor imagine for a moment, was the strange and beautiful pleasure I feel in life, in the midst of all this danger and death. I notice the beauty and delight of things far more than ever before. And, in the periods of comparative quiet, I take pleasure in almost every detail connected with being alive and the most ordinary and everyday things.

It gives me a thrill of delight to look at a golden-brown lemon pie that I have just baked; the homemade bread just out of the oven; a successful pudding; the pomegranate flowers on the tree outside the kitchen window; the absurd antics of Jemima and Keren, who scratch about the garden entirely undisturbed by exploding shells and shrapnel; the queer, ugly pigeon babies who so surprised me when in one day their porcupine quills unfurled into feathers. All these things and countless others, especially the kindness and goodness of Ruth, Ronald, Lilly, and Mrs. Gibson, give a pleasure and content and active delight I have never before experienced, just by very contrast to all horrors around.

On Sunday while we were at Communion, my eyes kept straying through the open door into the garden, where the sun was shining hotly on the tree beside the gatehouse, gilding the bare trunk and the dry earth with glory, and it gave me a thrill every time. Our Lord himself who was offering us his broken body and poured out blood, is the Maker of all these things, and the world around us is so beautiful because he made it so. It is strange and wonderful to be alive.

In the afternoon as I laid the table for tea, I thought how nice it looked with jam and chocolate buns. To add to the pleasure, Aili came in with Mutti and they had tea with us while we chatted and shared the news. Heavy shelling started again quite near us, and we persuaded them to wait a bit longer. Then it was quieter again. Yehuda, the man who pumps for us and empties the garbage bin, arrived as Aili and Mutti left. Ruth went downstairs with them to the front door, and Ronald went out with Yehuda. Charles and I were left alone in the kitchen.

Suddenly a series of tremendous explosions occurred, apparently exactly overhead. I felt paralyzed with fright as they crashed down one after the other. I dared not run downstairs; it felt as though the roof must fall at any moment.

Finally they ceased, and I moved towards the stairs with my legs shaking. I heard Ruth calling me: "Hannah, come down, come down quickly. Someone has been hit. I am afraid it is Yehuda." For a moment I could not move and then went to the front door. Ruth stood there wringing her hands.

Just inside our gate, nearly on the doorstep, lay Yehuda, facing us, resting on one hand, blood spattered all over him.

I shall never forget the stunned look of horror on his face and the pitiful beseeching way he looked at us without a word.

Then I saw Ronald running towards us and with him two of the splendid young stretcher bearers who worked with the ambulances. I thought one of them called reassuringly, "Oh, he is not much hurt." They lifted him up to put him on the stretcher, and as they did so, we saw what had happened and knew that he could not live. Ronald went with him across the garden to the Red Shield station. He said the doctors were magnificent and started a blood transfusion at once. Ronald stood by Yehuda holding his hand, but he died before they could operate.

It seems that Ronald had just turned the corner by our pump when it happened, and seeing Yehuda fall, he ran at once for help. Later we heard that Aili and Mutti had left our door and met Yehuda and just gone through the gate, when the shell crashed down. They threw themselves flat on the ground the other side of the fence a few feet away from where he fell.

When the stretcher bearers had gone, Ruth and I, feeling sick and queer, investigated the damage in the house. It was surprisingly little. Ronald's room just inside the front door suffered the most. Jagged pieces of shell had been hurled inside and plaster, of course, had fallen everywhere.

It was a relief to work. We all three started on the mess in Ronald's room and cleared that up, then the chapel, then the sitting room. Then I got the supper, and afterwards we set to work again. Ruth pasted gauze on the skylights and windows, and I rearranged the storeroom. Then we carried our beds in there, as it is an inner room with no outside windows. The shelling was bad in the night and again next morning, so I cooked downstairs.

June 9

Today the firing is further away. I cooked upstairs, and we had lunch up there in the air and light. We have hopes that a month's cease-fire is to start on Friday at 10:00 A.M. How we do pray for Count Bernadotte, the mediator, and ask that God will prosper his efforts for peace. It did seem unlikely that the Arabs would agree to lift the siege of Jerusalem, when report has it that we have only enough supplies left for one month. But the mediator proposes that the Red Cross shall feed the Jewish population in Jerusalem for one month. Immigration and entrance of Jews from Cyprus seem the main obstacles still, but rumor has it that Count Bernadotte has a solution for this too. It will indeed be wonderful to have a cease-fire, even if it is only for one month. Perhaps during that time they will be able to work out some plan to which both parties will agree.

We have heard from the consulate that we can each send two telegraphs a week (five words only) to our friends in England. What a relief this will be, after no communications of any kind for over a month.

June 13

Friday, June 11, was a great day for us. Exactly four weeks after the mandate ended there was a cease-fire all over Palestine. It is to last a month. This is due to Count Bernadotte, the mediator, who will have a staff of U.N. observers to implement the truce. It seems more like four months than four weeks of continual shelling that we have been through.

There was a local cease-fire in Jerusalem last Thursday from 8:00 A.M. till 2:00 P.M. while a Red Cross convoy got away. But just after 2:00 P.M. the shelling started again, and it was very bad in the night. So although the radio

said that both Jews and Arabs had agreed to Count Bernadotte's proposals, we hardly dared let ourselves hope
that it would really happen. Friday morning, June 11,
was dreadful; continual shelling right up to 10:00 A.M.,
and at least twenty people were killed that very morning.
One of Lilly's acquaintances was killed just a few moments
before 10:00 A.M.

But at 10:00 A.M. the truce really did happen. The crashes
died away, and Jerusalem became again, at least temporarily, a city of peace after seven months of continual war.

It is a strange and wonderful feeling to be able to stand
near windows and go outside and even sit in the garden or
on the rooftop. I began working as usual, behind closed
shutters, until I remembered and opened the door and went
out on the veranda. Even washing the sheets, a grueling
business, was delightful. I stood in the sunshine and the west
wind; the sky was heavenly blue, the birds sang, and there
was no death swooping down out of the sky. My heart sang
for joy. But there were many for whom the cease-fire came
too late. Some of the mourners for the morning's victims
were weeping and shrieking in the eastern style in the hospital grounds just below the veranda.

About midday (two hours after the cease-fire) we heard
an airplane. I went outside and looked up, and there circling
low over Jerusalem, just clearing the treetops, was a shining
white airplane bearing three huge red crosses. Somehow as
I stared up at that white messenger of hope flying over this
tormented city, telling us that we were under Red Cross protection and that Red Cross convoys would be bringing food,
I found my eyes full of tears.

The three crosses lifted up over Jerusalem. The symbol of
the rejected Christ. O Israel, if you only knew the things
that belong to your peace! This blessed temporary peace has

come to us because the Mediator has been at work, and God has granted him a measure of success. For one month at least, Jewish Jerusalem is to rest from her warfare, because she is under the protection of that symbol of the Christ she rejected. Oh, that they might turn to him and find lasting peace!

8

The Narrow Plain of Ease

With the arrival of the blessed cease-fire and the entry of the Red Cross food convoys, Jerusalem became a transformed city. The shops that had been closed for nearly a month reopened. The emptied streets were again thronged with citizens rejoicing in the light and air and in being able to move about freely without sudden destruction descending on them from the sky.

The first food convoy came through about June 20. As I hopefully sallied forth to try and do some shopping, I caught sight of Lilly standing at her gate, staring as one in a trance and so oblivious of everything that she did not even notice when I hailed her. On going up to her to ask what was the matter, she said, almost in a tone of ecstasy, "Oh, look, Hanah, there is a vegetable cart," and she pointed to a man pushing a small wheelbarrow to his shop containing tomatoes, potatoes, and onions. We hadn't seen a vegetable cart in the streets of Jerusalem since December—over six months ago.

As long as Jerusalem was besieged and food was dribbling into the city at the cost of the lifeblood of Jewish drivers and soldiers, we had not felt willing to draw even the tiny rations available, as we had stores of our own. But now that Red Cross convoys were bringing in supplies, we felt free to use our ration cards and draw our share of fresh fruit and vegetables. The first ration consisted of one tomato, one cucumber, and two onions for each person. I carried our three portions home in a string bag, feeling almost unbelievably happy.

For a whole month we had scarcely ventured out into the streets, and only now did we really begin to find out how others had fared and what life was like in a general way. Besides the shortage of food (which, however, had not been too acute owing to careful rationing), the continuous shelling and fighting, the day and night suffering of the wounded, and the widespread bereavement (for scarcely a family in Jerusalem escaped some loss), three main factors had added to the hardships endured by the people.

First, the Arabs had completely cut the water supply. Water has always been the major problem of this city situated on the top of the Judean hills, but to be cut off from the municipal supply during the rainless summer months did indeed look as though the Jewish area was doomed.

The Jewish authorities, however, had foreseen this and managed magnificently. What they accomplished did indeed seem like a miracle. As soon as the mandate ended, the Jewish forces concentrated on seizing the large outlying areas of the city that had been evacuated by Arabs and foreigners

who had fled the country. These suburbs were now cordoned off as military occupied zones. Most of the large,
pleasant houses in these zones were built in the old days
before Jerusalem had a municipal water supply and were
provided with large cisterns to conserve the winter rainfall.
All these cisterns in the evacuated zones were now carefully
tested, chlorinated, and sealed. All cisterns in the Jewish
area were treated in the same way and were locked and
sealed by the authorities.

Thus carefully preserved, the cistern water was then
strictly rationed out day by day, a small gas canful per person. Carts with pipes attached toured each area, and people
lined up, at first for hours, in the blazing sun, with empty
tins and buckets to receive their share. But when the shelling was severe, so many people in lines were killed that the
scheme was reorganized. Water carts came round to every
area at stated times, and the people collected the water more
or less at their own doors.

But even so, all of the water had to be carried by hand,
and those who lived in flats three or four stories high had a
terribly hard time. They erected pulleys and hauled up pails
by ropes, but of course much water splashed over and was
lost. Everybody worked at this job. Children carried jugs
and small tins, and even tiny tots carried a cupful.

A small tin for each person a day—for cooking, washing,
and laundry—is very little. People with large families came
off best, as their supply went further. Pamphlets were
printed telling people how to apportion the ration and make
the utmost use of it. This difficult situation went on for
months, although one point in the agreed cease-fire was that
the Arabs were to allow water to flow into Jerusalem for
that one month. In practice they utterly refused to do so and

finally blew up the Latrun pumping station, so as to make the flow of water to the city an impossibility.

However, by using the available cistern water as described, the population was able to carry on, if not comfortably, at least safely. It was always amazing to me to notice the well-laundered dresses and blouses of the women and the healthy, clean appearance of everyone. The Ramallah radio (Arabic) broadcast a report purporting to describe the appalling conditions in Jewish Jerusalem, due to the absence of water. It spoke of crowds of filthy, dejected people in the streets, vermin-infested garments, and people thirsty, nearly to despair. I couldn't help laughing as I listened to this travesty of the actual position and then compared it with the reality. No one who lived in Jewish Jerusalem through the summer of 1948 could fail to be impressed by the courage and calmness of the people as a whole. By October the authorities had succeeded in getting water piped to the city from another source, and the situation eased a little.

The second outstandingly difficult factor was the shortage of fuel and the failure of electricity. In some ways this was worse than the shortage of water, as that at least was adequate, though very restricted. But the absence of kerosene and electricity meant that Jerusalem was left with no means of cooking. The Judean mountains are practically treeless, and bundles of wood and Arab-made charcoal were no longer available. Fortunate people who had packing cases split them up to boil water once a day, while others used anything they could lay their hands on. Occasionally in some areas the electricity came on for an hour or two in the night. Then the housewives rushed from their beds, plugged in electric rings and kettles, cooked a little, and poured hot drinks into thermos flasks, if they had them, for use in the daytime, while daughters hastily did a little ironing of dresses and blouses. But the hardship that entailed on many who had no fuel at all was terrible, and this must be borne in mind as an explanation of what happened when the first truce began.

As so many prosperous suburbs of Jerusalem were now almost uninhabited, all the Arab and foreign population having moved or left the country, fueless people, in desperation, began to surge into those areas in search of wood for fuel from the gardens and homes of their departed enemies. Jewish houses in the Arab-occupied areas had already been looted and stripped of everything, and now the same process took place in these abandoned Arab homes. Everything valuable was taken, and everything able to be burned and used as fuel, went as well: shelves, cupboards, window frames, bookcases, tables, and chairs.

This looting was checked as much as possible, but desperate people searching for wood and stores surged into these areas night after night. When the Jerusalem Electric Company resumed a better supply of electricity and the situation was somewhat eased, sterner measures were taken to prevent these desperate looters from getting into the unoccupied zones. The few foreigners, Greeks and Armenians, etc., who had elected to remain in their homes were left unharmed and were able to guard their property. But empty houses were looked upon as lawful prey, belonging to enemies who had fled.

A third cause of strain and hardship for the population was the fact that so many people had been made homeless and now had to be distributed in other people's houses. All the women and children from the Jewish quarter of the Old City had been evacuated to the new. Rooms had to be found for them, while hundreds of families all around the borders of the New City had lost their homes.

There were wide areas of no-man's-land, in which both sides blew up as many buildings as possible to prevent the enemy from using them as bases for attack and for sniping. The border areas were unsafe to live in so that hundreds of families had to find new living quarters. Besides this, New Jerusalem is a city of flats, and the buildings are many stories high. Those who lived in upper flats, as well as the many poor who inhabited ancient, rickety buildings or dilapidated houses, always had to sleep at night in the basements or ground-floor rooms of obliging neighbors. This naturally was a constant strain and difficulty.

In spite of all this, however, it was wonderful to see how bravely and cheerfully the population carried on. The eastern Jewesses certainly, according to their ancient custom, shrieked and wailed and tore their hair at every death. The hospitals often sounded like bedlam while this was going on, but the younger generation and the European Jews behaved with wonderful quietness and heroism — even those who were most afraid. So that, apart from the shell holes in the roads and pavement, the battered shops and gaping windows and water lines, no one would have suspected, as soon as the cease-fire started, that Jerusalem had been in a state of virtual siege for seven months and had just come through a month's ordeal of fire.

As one walked about the city, which having been built on a series of hills commands wide views over the different areas, it was interesting to notice what a city of flags it had become. Not only the consulates, but every foreign-owned building displayed its national flag, and every nation in the world seemed represented. French flags were everywhere — on convents, schools, and churches; the American Stars and

Stripes fluttered high over other buildings, including the tower of the YMCA; the Red Cross flag and the flag of the United Nations could also be seen. Jerusalem boasts an almost unlimited number of consulates, and flags of Turkey, Greece, Belgium, Holland, Italy, etc., fluttered in every direction.

Only one flag seemed missing. The British consulate was out of sight in the Arab area, and nowhere was a Union Jack visible. The one flag that for so long had dominated the scene was now conspicuous by its absence. But it must be recorded with honesty and deep gratitude that however violent anti-British popular opinion was, we ourselves never once received a discourteous word, nor were we molested in any way. In shops, in lines, and in buses, everyone was kind, helpful, and friendly. They did not always disguise their views on Britain's policy, nor their indignation that Britain, as they claimed, supported the Arab legion in the war and supplied it with arms and officers. But, they seemed to try in every way to make it as easy for us as possible. Ruth was, of course, widely known as the beloved headmistress of a school where several generations of Jewish girls had received their education, and she was welcomed on all sides. Ronald, with his clerical collar, was recognizable anywhere. We had been permitted to remain as residents and were cordially welcomed as such. Having stayed to share the dangers (though from our specially favored position on the hospital compound we escaped many of the hardships), we were treated as friends and real members of the community. We often marveled at the kindness and helpfulness shown us on all sides.

Lilly came this afternoon (June 13) for our Friday prayer time together, and we gave thanks, remembering the Lord's promise: "I shall not die but live and declare the wonderful works of the Lord." In Jerusalem alone, more than four hundred civilians lost their lives in those four weeks. We are not told, of course, what the army casualties have been, here and on other fronts.

How real and comforting Psalm 91 has been during these weeks in the valley of the shadow of death, with the terror by night and the shells that fell by day. I do not of course suggest that God has any favorites, but I do acknowledge with deep gratitude and wondering awe that our Lord is of very tender compassion to those who are afraid. For Ronald has had shrapnel in his room, and Ruth and Lilly have had bullets in theirs, but nothing has touched my room and not even a picture has been shaken from the walls, as though in that gentle way the Lord would rebuke my fears.

Life in besieged Jerusalem has not been too easy for our little flock of livestock. There have been one or two minor tragedies in the henhouse. Famished dogs and cats are everywhere, and on Thursday a cat managed to get into the pigeon-house and ate the little gray mother and one of her eggs. Happily, the brown pigeons and their two squeakers escaped. I carried the poor, moping father outside and set him free and hope he will find a mate among all the wild pigeons that nest under the hospital eaves.

Then a huge and horrible dog keeps bursting into the garden and chasing Jemima and Keren-Happuch. Yesterday I was sure Keren had been killed: There was only a terrified Jemima and, nearby, a heap of black feathers. Poor dear, indefatigable, egg-producing Keren, and poor Jemima, her devoted companion, now left all alone! But at 7:00 P.M., as I went disconsolately out into the garden to see if Jemima was recovering from her fright, I turned a corner and saw a small black figure advancing meditatively towards me, and there was Keren-Happuch, safe and sound, returning to the fold. With what joy I welcomed her. But again this afternoon, this hateful dog got in. His mouth was full of feathers, and I was only just in time to rescue Keren, minus her tail, and Jemima with a bare, bleeding patch on her back.

But in spite of all this harrying they continue to lay their daily eggs, which I have to go and retrieve as soon as they proclaim the fact or famished cats enter the nest and suck the eggs dry. Ownerless cats and dogs have indeed had a hard time during this hungry period. The health department is killing off stray dogs, for fear of an outbreak of rabies. But cats are left as a prophylactic against plague-carrying rats. With so many foreign armies around Jerusalem, epidemics and plagues of all sorts are much to be feared.

June 30

I can scarcely believe it is true, but I am actually sitting under an olive tree in the open, having a quiet prayer afternoon. It is half a year or more since such a thing happened, except for the four days at Nablus. Last Sunday I decided I would try and get through to St. Andrew's Church, in the occupied zone, and see the Scottish minister and glean a little news of that end. For it has often seemed to us as though, living in the Jewish area of Jerusalem, we were on some distant planet, out of reach and out of touch with any other part of the earth.

To my joy and surprise, the Hagana guards at the barrier courteously allowed me to pass through and pay my visit, and I found myself alone on the open road between the Jewish area and the old German colony. There were no houses beside the road, just wasteland, with olive trees and towering thistles, and a glorious view of the mountains of Transjordan.

I found the Scottish minister all alone. His two Arab men-servants had been arrested and interned. The Scottish church, hospice, and manse look right out on the walls of the Old City across the valley and, thus, were in the very front line of the fire. For a whole month he had scarcely been able to venture outside the front of the house. He had no electricity, no radio, no papers, and no news. He had only heard of the proposed cease-fire by chance.

He had remained as sole guard of the property and lived there alone with his dog and fowls. Looters were an ever-present problem. He told me that the British families had left as soon as the cease-fire started. The Greeks, Armenians, and others who remained were protected by the Hagana and their property respected, but they were only free to move about for a few hours each day and could not leave the colony. He was still able to have a service on Sundays, though those who came had to run the gauntlet of shells and sniping.

As I listened to his account, I felt doubly thankful for our happy home at the hospital, the constant companionship of Ruth and Ronald, and the fellowship of our little Christian group. We had never been really without news or papers, and we were able to move about quite freely all over the Jewish area.

Walking home after the visit, it occurred to me that during the cease-fire I could do the one thing I longed for above everything else—spend a quiet afternoon of prayer out in the open under the trees. For here on either side of this deserted main road was a stretch of open land and olive trees and scarcely anyone about. I could bring a picnic tea one afternoon and pretend I was really out in the country and free once more.

So I have come this afternoon and am sitting in a kind of glen, a low place with olive trees and full of very prickly giant thistles. In the far distance, like a dream, I see the mountains of Moab. They look beautiful and tempting, but I am glad I am not there, for they are outside my Promised Land. How happy I am to be here, to be able to say like Abraham on nearby Mount Moriah, "Behold here I am, in the place thou didst send me to, doing the thing thou didst ask me to do."

Indeed what a difference it does make, having remained here in Jerusalem voluntarily. Perhaps if the mission had asked us to stay, or I had remained from a sense of duty, I would always be counting up the discomforts and dangers and reckoning myself hardly used. As it is, staying on of one's own free will because it is the Lord's choice, I can only count up all his loving kindnesses and daily tender mercies and feel how blessed I am.

Straight in front of me in the near foreground lies Mount Zion and Bishop Gobat School. And there, hoary with age, are the battlements and walls of the Old City, the Tower of David, and Jaffa Gate. And just out of sight behind the citadel is the mission compound. If I had wings it would be one minute's flight to land in the courtyard, and yet it is as far away as the other end of the world.

Across the valley I can hear the clocks in the Old City chiming and striking the hour. When the first clock began to strike, I glanced at my watch and saw that it said 5:00 P.M. Our friends would just have finished tea in the hostel lounge. Idly I listened to the number of strokes and started with surprise when it stopped at three. Then I remembered the great gulf fixed between New Jerusalem and the Old City, a gulf even of time, for our clocks are two hours in advance of theirs. That one simple matter of the clock that only struck three times seemed to emphasize afresh that in spite of the apparent peacefulness of the scene, we were as cut off from the friends just across the little valley as though we were in separate countries.

In some ways the two weeks since the cease-fire have been more trying than the weeks of actual fighting. Others say the same thing. Then we were keyed up and braced to bear whatever might come, but now that the danger is over we have all unconsciously relaxed. I suppose there is some kind of reaction, for I find that all sorts of little things get on my nerves and try me dreadfully.

During the cease-fire, as the school term had finished, we acceded to the earnest request of the hospital authorities to let them use nearly all our downstairs flat as a hospital for sick babies. So now we have thirty tiny babies with a staff of doctors and nurses downstairs. Some of our friends commiserated with us and said we little knew what a noisy time, day and night, we had let ourselves in for. But inside our own rooms the noise is not very noticeable, and we ourselves are already accustomed to it. But for nearly a week we have had no water in our taps because it was all drawn off downstairs. It is such a heavy and laborious labor pumping up water from our cistern into the tank on the roof, and to have it all drawn off before we can use it is very trying, though having no water in their taps is only what everyone else has had to endure for weeks.

But I get very impatient if Ronald forgets to fill the kitchen jugs and when he and Ruth come a little late to meals. I scold stridently when cats eat our precious daily egg for there are none to be bought in Jerusalem, and when dogs chase our hens and tear their feathers out, I shed tears of wrath and indignation. Ronald, the most kind and patient of young men, has traced the owner of the dog, so that particular menace now seems removed.

I do hate myself when I scold and get impatient. Yet when I consider the difficulties and strain we have been through, I think perhaps it is wonderful that the Lord keeps us as peaceful and happy as he does. I do not excuse myself and I do ask for grace to overcome exasperation, but I begin to feel that the Lord has applied more grace than I supposed.

Certainly he has given it abundantly to Ruth and Ronald. Ruth has been running the school under fearful difficulties, with the children needing to take shelter constantly, and she has been in continual anxiety for their safety. I am doing work I was never accustomed to and under abnormal conditions. Yet we still manage to enjoy it and keep wonderfully well and fit. Yes, I must confess that indeed our Lord has done wonders for us.

That was the only time it was possible to spend a quiet afternoon in the open. The next time I tried to visit the Scottish church I had to turn back. Sniping had restarted, and a perfect volley of bullets came whizzing up the main road. I saw a party of Jewish soldiers practically crawling up the streets to avoid these bullets, so I had to hurry into the nearest building to take shelter and realized that I must turn back. After that, when Ronald or I visited the Scottish church, we went on bicycles, made a detour of several miles, and finally walked a quarter of a mile up the deserted railway line and through the shelled station, and so crept into the hospice garden from the back. And always we had to obtain a special pass.

The cease-fire lasted four weeks.

9

Resumed Fighting and Second Truce

July 9

Today we begin the third page of Palestine's new chapter. Two pages are written already: the month of fighting and the month of truce. Today the fighting is to start again. Yesterday in the Jewish area, we were all strung up, waiting to hear what answer the leaders of both sides would give to Count Bernadotte's request for an extension of the cease-fire. The streets were full of worried, silent people. Sometimes friends said to us, "I shall go mad if it starts again," or "I can't bear it."

We broke off our 6:00 P.M. Bible class in order to hear the BBC news. Ruth knelt in front of the radio, intending to hear every word. But we had forgotten for the moment that we were four hours in advance of London time, and there was no news bulletin after all. At 8:00 P.M. we did hear the news, which said that the Jews had agreed to an extension of the truce, but the Arabs had rejected it.

The cease-fire is to end today at noon. The Arabs did not agree to even a three-day extension to allow the U.N. observers to leave Jerusalem in safety, so they all left yesterday. We hear that already fierce fighting has restarted in southern Palestine.

Yesterday we were busy finishing as many jobs as possible, especially washing sheets and doing the laundry. In the evening I went up on the roof for the last time, to have a quiet hour with the Lord. There was a huge fire blazing near Schneller's School, crimsoning the sky, a bad omen of another conflagration about to break out again. I did not know how to face the thought of going through all that dreadful ordeal again, and I just fled to him for refuge. How do people manage without him in times like these?

This morning when I got up and went out to feed the chickens as usual, I saw Charles lying on the floor, waiting to go with me, and I exclaimed, "Oh, poor old Charles, this is a bad day for us today." And then in a flash I remembered the text Frank Boreham writes of in one of his books. He had seen it written with a diamond on the window in old Bessie's cottage.

"This is the day the Lord hath made, we will be glad to rejoice in it." And I exclaimed, "Oh, how could I say such a dreadful thing! Our Lord has made this day, too, so it can't really be bad, whatever happens." And I opened Frank Boreham's book and read again that lovely incident and felt so comforted.

Old Bessie said, "It occurred to me that the text means any day, every day. *This* is the day the Lord hath made. . . . Somehow you don't feel afraid of the day if you know that he made it." And Boreham added, "since this little world first swung in space, there never has come a day of which you could not sing, 'This is the day the Lord hath made, we will be glad and rejoice in it.' . . . Nobody but God would dare to make a day . . . he dares because he knows that he is mighty enough to control it."

Today unless God intervenes with a miracle, we must go back into the valley of the shadow of death. But this is the day the Lord has made, even as every tomorrow will be, and I *will* be glad and rejoice in it. Thank God we start in health and strength, and as far as possible with everything ready. Psalm 91 and Psalm 118 are still his Word to me.

Later

We were busy all of the morning. Ronald escorted Mr. and Mrs. Datzi to the YMCA to be under Red Cross protection. Then he and Ruth cleared the cellars, as the babies needed a shelter. I was busy in the kitchen, baking bread and cooking and doing the ironing. It was far worse waiting for the resumption of hostilities than the first time. Then we didn't know what to expect. Now we knew only too well. I felt frightened but kept on thinking, *This is the day the Lord has made, and he is in control* and felt better.

Just a few minutes before the time that had been fixed, at midday, we heard it all begin again, first shots and then mortars. At 12:20 P.M. the first ambulance rushed in with the wounded. Back in the valley of the shadow, I still find myself able to sing, "I will fear no evil, for *thou* art with me."

It is Friday again, a red-letter day every week, for Lilly and I meet together for a prayer afternoon. It is wonderful how such times renew and strengthen us, physically as well as spiritually. I am glad Friday is the afternoon we fixed on each week. Somehow specially significant things seem to happen on Fridays, and it is good to meet them with prayer. The British Mandate ended and the state of Israel was born on a Friday. The first cease-fire came into effect on a Friday, and so did this resumption of hostilities. When we meet together this afternoon, how much we shall have to praise for and how much to pray about.

July 11

Alas, I find myself very nervous now that the shelling has started again and seems to be getting nearer. By supper time on the very first evening the mortars had started. They were not very close, but the feeling that at any moment they might get in our range again was horrid. We all seem to find it worse than we did before.

While we were having our weekly staff prayer meeting, the shooting was near, and bullets whizzed past the windows. As we knelt there in our little sitting room, I did very earnestly ask the Lord to take my fear away, that if it be his will I might stop *feeling* afraid, because fear does have such torment. If I really believed his promises, I would know nothing could touch us, and if I were selfless and fully surrendered, I would not shrink at the thought of being hit, knowing it would be only because he allowed it.

It is not being killed that I fear, but being wounded and maimed, and the suffering one would go through. *But O Lord Jesus, do work a real change in me, that I may think of others much more, and not of myself, and that I may really rest on thy word, and know that thou wilt honor thy promises.* "He shall cover thee with his feathers, and under his wings shalt thou trust" (Ps. 91:4).

July 12

On the night of July 9, Jerusalem had its first air raid in history. Fortunately hardly any damage was done. Today *Daily Light* is very lovely and comforting for these hard days: "Be strong and of good courage. Fear not nor be afraid. Have not I commanded thee? Be strong and of a good courage, be not afraid neither be dismayed, for the Lord thy God is with thee. He hath said, 'I will never leave thee nor forsake thee.'"

Hudson Taylor once said, "God's commands are his enablings. When he said, 'Let there be light, there was light.' All his commands are like that. So when he says, 'Be strong and of good courage, be not afraid,' it must work in the same way, and fear goes."

July 15

God has brought us safely through the worst night so far. Since the end of the cease-fire, the Jews have made tremendous military gains, taking Lydda, Ramleh, and the Ras el Ain pumping station. Yesterday they took Shefa'mr, near Haifa. For a time Jerusalem was comparatively quiet, though nasty shells came crashing down at odd moments without any warning.

But last night at 9:00 P.M. a terrific barrage began with hundred pounders, and we went down once more to sleep in the storeroom. At 11:00 P.M. still heavier shelling started. There were crashes all around, and of course the light went, while a horrible plane circled around, dropping bombs every now and then. As Jerusalem has no antiaircraft guns, a bomber sneaking about overhead with nothing to drive it away is not at all pleasant. Hour after hour we lay in the darkness, listening to the shells being fired then coming towards us, and then crashing down. The noise was dreadful, but I lay in bed, thinking of the Lord's lovely, reassuring words in *Daily Light*, "Have not I commanded thee . . . be not afraid."

Charles, too, is a great help to me. The Lord has been teaching me many things through this funny little dog. Charles hates shells as much as I do, but he will never leave me for a moment, even when I go into the garden, though shells are worse out of doors than inside. At night when the shelling is heavy, I let him get up on the foot of my bed. With every crash that comes, he wriggles a little higher up the bed until at last he is at the top, and I put my arms around him. Then he heaves a great sigh of relief, his little body stops trembling, and he falls fast asleep and takes no more notice of the shells. If a little dog can trust me like that, how much easier it ought to be for me to trust such a loving and mighty Lord.

July 17

On the rooftop again. Our wonderful God has worked once more, and after passing through the worst day and night of all, the seemingly impossible has happened. There is a second cease-fire, which is supposed to be permanent, and Jerusalem, we hope, is to be demilitarized. It seems unbelievable.

The Security Council, at last, by eight votes out of eleven, has ordered both sides to cease-fire permanently, on penalty of incurring sanctions. The cease-fire all over Palestine is to start on Monday, and in Jerusalem, within twenty-four hours. The Jews agreed, while the Arabs strongly objected.

Wednesday night was dreadful, so on Thursday everybody stayed indoors with the result that not so many were hurt. But Thursday night was almost perfectly quiet. We slept peacefully and people crowded thankfully out into the

streets on Friday morning to do their weekend shopping. At
9:30 A.M., when almost everybody had been tempted out by
the quietness, an appalling bombardment started and lasted
all day and all night. These shells seem to explode in the air
and descend in a deadly rain of shrapnel, but they do not
really damage well-made buildings. We feared many were
wounded and killed, and the wailing for the dead around the
hospitals was very sad. Also there was much shooting, and a
bullet came into our kitchen.

We hung about the radio all day long, hoping to hear the
Arab decision, as the cease-fire in Jerusalem was scheduled
to begin at 5:30 A.M. the next morning (Saturday). But by
10:00 P.M. on Friday the Arabs still had not announced their
decision.

As it was Friday, Lilly came to tea, and we had our
weekly prayer time. Fridays are indeed momentous days.
Shells were still crashing down, but God gave us great liberty to believe and claim that he had "shortened the time"
and the cease-fire would actually take place. Then I went
home with Lilly, and Mrs. Gibson showed me how to make
mayonnaise. A moment before I started to leave, an appalling crash occurred just overhead, then two more. I ran for
my life, waving a jug of mayonnaise in one hand and an egg-
beater in the other, and got back to our house just before the
next batch of shells got in our range. I found the nurses carrying the babies down to the cellar, and Ruth and Ronald
feeling as though they had just been concussed.

It was by far the worst night of all. Both sides seemed to
be wanting to use up all their unused shells and trying to
advance their positions so as to have as much to bargain
with as possible.

All night long, without cessation, the shells came crashing
over in a steady stream, each one sounding and feeling as

though it had exploded exactly overhead. Mortars crashed and guns belched; bullets hissed and crackled on the walls. Every now and then the walls rocked and doors burst open, and we knew that houses and buildings were being blown up. The babies in the cellar wailed and screamed. The ghostly nurses flitted through the storeroom where our beds were, as the only inside cellar stairs are there. We lay cowering in bed with our nerves taut, listening to the shells starting out from Nebi Samwil and waiting for their arrival. I lay repeating to myself, "A thousand shall fall at thy side, and ten thousand at thy right hand, but it shall not come nigh thee." At last, hearing Ruth catch her breath as she lay in the bed beside mine, I repeated the verse aloud, meaning to share my morsel of comfort. Ruth's reaction was quite unexpected. "I can't bear to think of a thousand poor people being killed and blown to bits, while I lie here quite safely," she burst out, "let alone ten thousand. I never did like that verse."

I felt terribly abashed, but after the next crash, ventured to suggest, "But do you think it means people? I thought David was referring to the ancient equivalent of shells. Though a thousand shells fall beside me, they will not be able to harm us."

"Oh," said Ruth, quite mollified, "if David meant arrows, that is much better. I never thought of it in that light before."

We still didn't know if the Arabs had agreed to cease-fire at 5:30 A.M. Soon after 4:00 A.M. I must have fallen asleep again in spite of the noise. At 6:20 A.M. I woke and there was blessed and wonderful silence. Instinctively I ran out quickly into the garden to feed the hens, in case the shelling started again. It was still dark. There was no electricity, no radio news, and no newspaper, but also, no firing.

At the end of the morning Ronald brought us the news that the Arabs had agreed to the cease-fire in Jerusalem, but had not decided about the rest of Palestine.

July 18

This morning at 5:00 A.M. there was a tremendous outbreak of shooting again—just as though there was no cease-fire—bullets, mortars, and crashes, and we all retired downstairs until 7:30 A.M. It is most disappointing, but of course until the mediator and his observers get back, there is no one to superintend the truce. We must hope for better things when they do arrive.

At 9:15 A.M. while we were at Communion, battle was still raging all around, and until now, midday, it has continued unabated. All this time the Arabs won't announce whether they agree to a cease-fire all over Palestine or not. It should start at 7:00 P.M. this evening. The Jews say that if the Arabs will not agree to this, they on their part will annul the Jerusalem truce. May God help us in that case. But of course he will.

The *Palestine Post* has announced that the five Britons from the Jerusalem Electric Corporation, who were arrested by the IZL (an illegal dissident group), are to be publicly tried for espionage and for having an unlicensed transmitter. It seems rather absurd since everybody knew about this transmitter, and we were all told the time they were to transmit greetings and personal messages to the Britishers in different parts of the city. Now we feel thankful nobody suggested leaving us a transmitter.

We hear that Nazareth has surrendered to the Israeli forces. Our thoughts go to our friends there at the mission hospital and the orphanage.

On July 18 the new Israel currency was introduced into the Jewish areas of Palestine, and a little later, new Israel postage stamps, with ancient Maccabean emblems on them.

July 19

He that is mighty hath done for us great things, and holy is his name.

All day yesterday the battle raged, and the radio kept announcing that the Arabs had not given their decision about the truce, but that Arab opinion was strongly in favor of continuing the war. As I was getting the supper, Ronald came in and said, "I am afraid things are pretty hopeless, and there seems no likelihood at all of a truce."

Later, as we were finishing supper, he went to the sitting room to hear the eight o'clock headlines. I said to Ruth, "I have a very strong feeling that God has overruled and there will be a cessation of hostilities. We were given such liberty to claim this during the prayer afternoon on Friday."

Ronald then came hurrying back with a beaming face and said, "Grand news. The Arabs have agreed to a truce all over Palestine, and King Abdullah has said that the matter cannot be settled by fighting, but by negotiation."

Only people who have been through battle and siege can know how we felt. We went immediately to the sitting room and knelt down and thanked God and rejoiced together. Then Ronald hurried out to tell others, as most people still had no electricity and so no radio. I rang up Mrs. Gibson and Lilly and told them the news. God had done wonderful things, just as he had promised.

With the arrival of this second truce, things in the Jewish part of the city gradually became more normal. Convoys came through, and the shops began to fill again. We got fresh vegetables and fruit, as well as tinned things—of course, all at wartime prices. But it was remarkable to see how quickly and bravely the people resumed their usual way of life.

The various municipal departments were splendid. The city was cleaned and cleared at last of glass and litter. Water was brought to every street, and was gradually pumped into the pipes. Life became much easier and pleasanter in every way. On July 20 I received the first letter from my home for three months, and by July 26 regular postal services were started between Israel and Great Britain.

On August 3 there was a ring at the door, and a beaming youth bustled in with a large basket of linen, which we had sent to the laundry at the beginning of May. The laundries had all been deprived of water directly afterwards, but now, three months later, everything was returned to us safe and sound.

The cease-fire itself was far from being perfect, especially in Jerusalem, which continued noisy and unsafe for months to come. The U.N. observers had a very busy time trying to establish responsibility for the frequent breaches of the truce, and these became more and more frequent as time went on. But we had a feeling that countrywide war had been more or less checked.

On August 12 we heard shocking news for Jerusalem. The Arabs had blown up the Latrun pumping station in order to prevent water reaching us, in defiance of the truce terms. The damage was too bad to be repaired for many months to come. This was a sad blow, as we had been daily expecting the resumption of the flow of water to the city.

On August 15 we were wakened by a dreadful battle just before 6:00 A.M.—shots, mortars, and explosions all over Jerusalem, till the whole city seemed rattling. It was the ninth of Ab (the anniversary of the destruction of the temple), and the Jews could not get to the wailing wall in the Old City, as was their custom. And of course they were justly incensed at the destruction of the Latrun pumping station, so everyone had been expecting some sort of outbreak. We heard that Count Bernadotte had left the Red Cross Conference in Sweden to return to his headquarters at Rhodes, as the situation in Palestine had become so serious and the truce was in such jeopardy.

Just before 4:00 A.M. on August 16, another dreadful battle started. It was so bad, I decided, coward that I was, to go downstairs, though the other two did not stir. However, I found the nurses trying to get to the cellars with twenty-six babies, so I helped them. We deposited all the babies on mattresses on the floor, five to a mattress, and very sweet and cherubic they looked, all swaddled and smiling toothlessly.

On August 28 the fighting in Jerusalem was worse than it had been at any time during the second truce. Two U.N. observers were killed, and an emergency message was sent to Count Bernadotte to say the situation in Jerusalem had deteriorated dangerously.

For several weeks we had been thinking about the possibility of getting some kind of holiday, but no one could leave Jerusalem without a special permit from the Jewish military authorities, and there was very little transport available. Now it was decided that Ronald should fly to England for a few weeks' holiday, Ruth was to go down to Tel Aviv, and when they both got back, I was to take my holiday.

Of course, the main road out of Jerusalem was still unusable, except for U.N. cars and Red Cross convoys, as the Arab legion was still sitting astride the road in the Latrun area. The Jews, however, had actually succeeded in making a rough track across the lower foothills, bypassing this fatal

Latrun area and connecting up with the main southern road to Tel Aviv. This new track was called the "Burma Road," and very rough going it was at that time, though Jewish engineers were constantly improving it. Ronald and Ruth were able to get permits to leave and also seats in one of the hospital ambulances, and on September 6 they left Jerusalem. It was a strange feeling, after seeing them off in the ambulance, to turn back alone to our home and to realize that as far as I knew I was the only British Christian in the Jewish area. But Lilly and Mrs. Gibson were still there, and it had been arranged that I should take my midday meal with them every day so that I should not be lonely.

But besides the happy companionship with them, there was another antidote to loneliness. I arranged a little shelter on the roof, protected from sun and wind. The tops of the pine trees in the hospital garden waved all round it and made a sea of green, where the birds twittered happily and the wild pigeons fluttered about and courted one another. To the north, far away over the housetops, there were glimpses of the mountains on which Ramallah is situated. And westward in the evenings the sun set in glory, and the pigeons wheeled about in flocks with their wings glittering like gold and silver. In this delightful little arbor I placed a small table, a chair for myself and a chair for Charles, and prepared to write this book. I used to carry my meals up there, too, and so spent most of the time in the open air, an unspeakable joy and relaxation.

I had high hopes of filling in the lonely weeks happily and profitably, but at first nothing happened as planned. I found that mentally I was very tired. My mind almost refused to concentrate on the work, and the interruptions were endless. Every time the doorbell or the telephone rang I had to leap downstairs. This happened almost constantly the first week, until people found out that Ronald and Ruth were away. Although the first week after their departure was comparatively quiet, everything happened with a rush afterwards, and we had two of the most sensational weeks of the summer.

On September 10 Jerusalem received its first ration of meat since the preceding December, 120 grams each person. Charles and I joined a very determined and hilarious line outside the butcher's shop and gradually worked our way inside and took our turn at the counter. Charles could scarcely believe the evidence of his nose, and when the butcher graciously tossed him a nugget of gristle about the size of a farthing, he was nearly transported with joy and astonishment. That was the only really pleasant event during a dreadful fortnight.

On September 11 and 12, after a week's lull, heavy shelling started again, and once more the ambulances were rushing to and from the hospital. The next day it was worse than at any time during either truce. Of course I could not possibly venture out on the rooftop.

On the thirteenth the Jewish schools reopened after the summer. That very first day a shell crashed down on the playground of the Alliance School, very near to the hospital, killing two children and wounding others. On the fourteenth I received news that many shells had fallen on and beside the mission compound in the Old City, while the Armenian quarter next door to the mission had been very badly damaged and many people killed. The maid at the mission hostel was also killed and her mother seriously wounded. A few weeks before, their nice Arab manservant had been killed by a shell on the mission compound.

On this same day the first Supreme Court of Israel was opened in Jerusalem. As I read the report of the speeches of the new chief justice, I could not help being very impressed. He quoted from the Talmud a description of the characteristics of a true judge and prayed that Israel might be blessed with righteous judges.

The next day, September 15, a poor woman arrived at our front door, spattered with blood and nearly hysterical. She asked if she could come in and sit down. Her neighbor had been walking along the street with her, when suddenly a sniper's bullet hit him in the head, and he dropped unconscious on the pavement. A passing van came to her rescue. She and the driver lifted him into the van and rushed him to the hospital. He was now on the operating table, and she was waiting to hear if they could save him. I sat with her for an hour while she drank tea, poured out the story over and over again, and gradually got over the shock.

On this same day, the trial started of the last of the two Britishers accused of espionage. The other three already had been acquitted. The following morning, one of the judges hearing the case dropped dead in the court. That night the wife of our retired hospital steward had another attack of cerebral hemorrhage, and the doctors said it would prove fatal. It was very sad to me that this should happen while Ronald and Ruth were away. That evening another appalling battle started. I was obliged to sleep down in the storeroom, not such a pleasant experience with no Ruth in the empty bed beside me, and no Ronald calling encouraging remarks through the open door of the next room.

The next day was Friday, September 17, another of those momentous Fridays. Lilly came for a prayer afternoon, and we took the tea tray up on the roof and sat in my little arbor, rejoicing in the view of distant mountains and open country and the lovely sunset colors. After she had left and I had eaten my supper, I turned on the radio to listen to the Arab news bulletin from Ramallah (it was always an intriguing experience to compare it with the Jewish news bulletin two hours later). In the middle of the news the announcer suddenly stopped, saying, "An urgent message has just been handed to me." A moment later he announced, "His Majesty King Abdullah of Transjordan wishes to express his horror and sorrow at the dreadful assassination of Count Bernadotte, the mediator, while in Jerusalem this morning."

The ground seemed to rock under me. It was utterly and horribly unbelievable. I sat on my bed and wept as though for a dear, personal friend. That our own mediator, for whom we had prayed so earnestly and from whose patient efforts for peace we had hoped for so much, should be killed while going about his work of trying to bring peace to this war-wrecked country seemed too frightful to be true. There was no Ruth or Ronald to turn to for comfort. I went to the phone and rang up the American church, and when Mrs. Gibson's voice answered, I told her the dreadful news. She was almost too sorrowful to speak, but it was a comfort just to have a friend to turn to at such a moment.

Later we heard the shocking news that the mediator had indeed been assassinated in cold blood, by Jews, members of the terrorist Stern Gang, while he was on a visit to the Jewish area of Jerusalem. Captain Cireau, one of the French observers, had been murdered at the same time. The Jewish liaison officer had done his utmost to save them and had rushed the car to this hospital, but by that time Count Bernadotte had died. I kept thinking of the Lord's lament over this city so long ago: "O Jerusalem, Jerusalem, thou that killest the prophets, and stonest them which are sent unto thee" (Matt. 23:37).

The whole world, including the Jewish community, was appalled by this shocking crime committed by the terrorists.

It did seem, indeed, that some of Israel's worst enemies were right in the midst of her. Nothing that her acknowledged enemies had done to her could so damage the Israel cause, as this crime committed by some of her so-called "patriots."

Next day, September 18, there was curfew all over the Jewish area, while the Israel police made raids and tried to find the assassins. A few days later the Israeli Government announced that all terrorist groups were illegal. The IZL and Stern Gang were disbanded, and many people suspected of being members of these groups were arrested.

After this dreadful event there was comparative quiet for a few days while police searches went on and both sides held their fire. The Burma Road was closed to all traffic to prevent the terrorists from escaping from Jerusalem. I began to be anxious about Ruth, who was due to return and now would be unable to get back to Jerusalem as long as the road was closed. I wondered if she would try to come with a U.N. convoy or with the Red Cross.

On September 19 there was another great battle in the Jerusalem area, and I ate my supper cowering in the passage behind double walls. At 10:00 P.M. on the twenty-third I was in bed, listening to the last news bulletin and wondering when Ruth would manage to get home again, when the announcer said that a convoy under U.N. protection had left Tel Aviv for Jerusalem, going by the main road as U.N. convoys always did. As they neared Latrun, the Arabs had opened fire on them. The U.N. observer in the first car got out waving the U.N. flag and heroically advanced towards the Arab soldiers, calling on them to cease firing. For answer, they shot again in his direction. The driver of his car then pushed a Jew, who was traveling with them, onto the floor and rushed, under fire, to the Latrun Monastery, where the monks hid the man and refused to give him up when Arabs came to search for him. Meanwhile the rear cars in the convoy had managed to turn around when the firing started and escaped back to Tel Aviv. But the first car behind the U.N. jeep could not do this. Its four occupants got out and threw themselves in a ditch. The Arabs then advanced and shot them dead while they lay there. One of the victims was a woman. No names were given.

The nameless woman victim in the ditch! Who was she? Surely it couldn't be Ruth? But I knew how anxious she would have been to get home to Jerusalem as soon as some way opened. Jewish traffic was still at a standstill, with the Burma Road closed. What more likely than that she should try to go with the U.N. convoy? I lay awake hours that night, always turning to that ditch in imagination and the four riddled bodies, one of them a woman's.

The next morning the radio still gave no names, but when the *Palestine Post* arrived a little later it reported that the woman who had been killed was a well-known Dutch lady, much beloved by a large circle of friends in Jerusalem. A little later a telegram arrived from Ruth, who guessed how anxious I would be, saying she would come as soon as the road reopened.

The next day, September 24, the wife of one of our hospital staff died. The matron of the Hadassah was very kind and helpful. The hospital lent us an ambulance for the funeral, as there was no other transport available. With a special permit from the Jewish military authorities, we took her to the little American cemetery in the half-deserted German colony. How thankful we were for this one Christian cemetery left inside the city. There were no cemeteries for the hundreds of Jewish dead. Since the end of the mandate, all who had been killed or died were put in coffins and were then taken to caves where the coffins were piled up waiting for proper burial after the war.

On September 26 we heard that nineteen decapitated Jewish bodies had been found near Lydda. On September 28 the new self-styled Arab government held its first meeting in Gaza. King Abdullah, as well as the Palestinian Arabs as a whole, appeared to be strongly opposed to this government with the ex-Mufti at its head. We were all glad to hear a few weeks later that, following Jewish victories in the Gaza area and the capture of Beersheba, this unwanted government had retired from Gaza to a quiet suburb in Cairo.

On the afternoon of September 29, to my unspeakable relief and comfort, Ruth arrived safely back from Tel Aviv, the Burma Road being once more open to Jewish traffic. She had only been away three weeks, but so much had happened during that time that it seemed like three months.

The following day blackout regulations came into force all over Israel. There were frequent air-raid warnings, but few if any bombs were dropped on Jerusalem.

After that we had a few days of comparative quiet, a rare phenomenon during truce number two. Then shelling started again in Jerusalem on October 6, and fighting all along the city's fronts. This went on day after day and night after night.

By October 16 fierce battles were raging in southern Palestine, as Jewish food convoys tried to get through to the settlements in the Negev. The first convoy was attacked and had to retreat with heavy casualties. This obstruction of the road by the Egyptians was a serious breach of the terms of the truce, and the Jews no longer felt bound to observe their side of the cease-fire. They started a strong offensive against the Egyptians and began to close in on Gaza. A little later fighting also broke out again in northern Palestine, and the

Syrian and Iraqi armies found themselves pressed back over the Syrian border.

On Sunday, October 17, there was a knock on the door. Charles broke into a loud outcry, and in walked Ronald, back from his four weeks in England. The family was once more complete. Of course, one never knew when people would arrive, traveling conditions were so uncertain, and post was delayed for weeks. How welcome a return it was, and we received him as a voyager from some other planet. He was dusty and tired from his journey up the Burma Road, but the first thing we did was to lead him to the pump, which after weeks of shocking deterioration, had at last become defunct. The day before, we had been unable to raise one single drop of water to the surface, though we swung the handle hundreds of times. We had only desisted from our despairing efforts when it became apparent that not only would no water appear, but that we ourselves would collapse beside the pump. By some sort of magical manipulation, Ronald succeeded in raising water and the next day even persuaded a plumber to come and put the pump in order.

Three days later, on October 20, the Jews took Beersheba, and the Egyptians were on the run.[6]

10 *A Moment of Peace*

*O*ctober 28 was a red-letter day, for after being shut up in besieged Jerusalem for seven months, I started off on my first visit outside the city since April and went to Haifa for a few weeks' holiday. It is quite impossible to describe the dreamlike sensations of amazement, joy, and curiosity with which I found myself actually traveling again and on the way to visit friends who for months had seemed so remote as to be in another world altogether. Indeed for the first week of the holiday I seemed to be in a dream the whole time, like someone returning to this world after exile on a distant planet.

By this time, most of the fighting had died down, the Israel forces proving greatly superior to their enemies on all fronts. But in Jerusalem there were still explosions and snipings. Most of the larger Arab towns in the country were now in Jewish hands (Jaffa, Lydda, Ramleh, Haifa, Beersheba, Tiberias, Nazareth, etc.), and only the large inland, mountainous triangle between Jenin, Tulkarm, and Ramallah remained solidly in the hands of the Arabs. There were no Jewish settlements in that area at all. The new Burma Road now connected Jewish Jerusalem with the rest of the Israel territory, while the Arab legion still held the main road in the Latrun area.

October 28

It was a great day yesterday when I got a seat in a taxi and left the city by the old familiar road, so long closed by fighting, and started down the mountains. Every Arab village that we passed was empty and deserted. Desperate battles had been raging for weeks in this area. The Arab armies entrenched themselves in the villages overlooking the main road, and did their utmost to prevent convoys bringing supplies to the city.

Qastal, especially, had been the scene of desperate and bloody battles, as it changed hands over and over again. It was a tiny Arab village of mud houses, on a pinnacle that dominated the main road in two directions at the very steepest part of the mountains. It was almost the last village that we had visited and preached in before the proclamation of partition had made travel impossible. A primitive, wretched little place, it was a mere collection of tiny mud houses inhabited by peasants working for a great landowner.

As we drove up the long, steep hill towards this strategic village, which was now a heap of ruins, I remembered how we had sat there on the floor in a smoke-blackened room, with no light coming in except through the door, and tried to preach to the womenfolk who were preparing food for a forthcoming wedding.

Still further on as we descended through the beautiful Bab il Wad, a winding ravine with steep, precipitous cliffs clothed with spruce and firs, we found the road lined with burned-out vehicles of all descriptions, bearing mute and terrible witness to the weeks and months when Israel was fighting to keep the road open for food convoys to Jerusalem.

At the foot of the mountains we left the main road, as only a few miles further on was the death trap around Latrun. Branching south, we came to the new and famous Burma Road. A great deal of it was already finished, but there were still a few miles of broken track where the dust swirled up in towering clouds so thick that nothing at all could be seen. Workmen were struggling desperately to finish the road before the winter rains set in and made an earth track impassable.

Toward the end of this Burma Road, and where it was still at its bumpiest, our taxi had to draw up behind a cavalcade of bumping cars. The foremost one displayed the Israeli flag, and before it went two uniformed outriders on motorcycles. Behind it was a police truck with half a dozen men in the uniforms of the ex-British police. For a moment a tiny pang shot through me as I remembered the days when this would have meant that the high commissioner was out on tour. But now we all leaned eagerly forward to see which of the Israeli leaders was being escorted, and my friendly fellow passengers, on catching sight of a gray trilby through the window and a lady's hat beside it, assured me it was Dr. Weizmann himself, the first president of the new State of Israel.

I would love to have caught a proper glimpse of this great and good man who has been one of the chief instruments in God's hands of making the new Jewish state possible, but one cannot "cut in" on a president. Though our driver did good-naturedly spurt forward and pass a carload of indignant press and one or two other vehicles, we were finally obliged to draw up behind a police truck and content ourselves with occasional glimpses of the gray trilby, till we got on to the main southern road, where we followed the president to his hometown of Rehovot, and then sped on to Tel Aviv. Here I had to change taxis but was fortunate enough to get a seat in one leaving for Haifa in fifteen minutes.

Being first and foremost a Galilean who now lives in Jerusalem, I never feel really at home in the Tel Aviv area of crowded suburban settlements that line the main road, with endless groves of orange trees in stiff, artificial rows. But when after an hour's driving we came to Hedera, it began to feel like home. There in the distance was Carmel, rugged and lovely. Gradually the range curved towards us and the plain narrowed between it and the sea. Then there were sand dunes with olive groves, beautiful and harmonious, replacing the oranges. As the sun set and the sea came nearly to the road, we rounded the last spur of Carmel, and with the usual shock of surprise at its loveliness, I saw Haifa, with its white buildings, and the misty mountains across the Bay of Acre. At 6:00 P.M. I clambered up the hill to the mission station and found myself welcomed back to the house I had first come to as a stranger seventeen years before.

Everything seemed outwardly unchanged in Haifa, as only brief fighting had occurred before the Jews occupied it completely. The majority of Arabs had left, but I heard that those who had remained were well treated and were busily learning Hebrew, not nearly such a difficult feat as for a European, as Arabic and Hebrew are both Semitic languages and are first cousins.

War seemed very far away in Haifa. The first morning, after the unexpected and delightful arrival of missionary friends who had come in on a shopping expedition from Israel-occupied Nazareth, I climbed the garden terraces to the shade of an old tree overlooking the Haifa Bay. How I did want to meet the Lord and begin the holiday with him, that it might all be spent with him. How I did pray that he would use those quiet weeks of rest, not only to fit and strengthen me for return to work, but that it might be a wonderful and priceless opportunity of going apart with him.

So much of vital and tremendous importance had happened in the country. The old order had changed and an amazing new one had started, and I did desperately need undisturbed time with him in which to become readjusted and reoriented to the new situation. There was so much I wanted to ask him about and to have explained to me. But most of all I prayed, "Give unto thy servant a hearing heart." God did abundantly answer this prayer.

Never in my life have I had any holiday so radiantly and continuously illuminated by his presence. Morning after morning I filled a bag with Bible and notebooks, and taking a thermos flask of tea and a packet of biscuits, climbed an old goat track up the side of Carmel behind the mission compound. Here was perfect solitude and the unspeakable delight of being able to wander about freely without fear of shooting or danger of any kind. It is true the sirens went quite often, and sometimes enemy planes circled over Haifa and the antiaircraft guns went into action, but no bombs seemed to be dropped. Halfway up the mountains a large pine tree stood beside the goat track, and in the shade of this pine tree I sat for three or four hours most mornings of that first three weeks, Haifa spread out at my feet, with the harbor, the bay, and the distant mountains.

During the first three weeks of November there was a continual, scorching east wind. It was not a beautiful time for a holiday, for it was the end of the long, rainless season. Everything was parched and withered, and a haze of heat enveloped the northern mountains, but nothing can make Carmel and the bay anything but beautiful, and the wide view was a never-ending joy. Day after day I watched the little immigrant ships sailing into the harbor; at last Jewish refugees and exiles were free to return to their own land. Everywhere one looked, there were signs and evidences of the new Israel, which (a miracle indeed) had come into being after nearly two thousand years of Israel's dispersion. At the end of the three weeks, the long dry season broke in rain and tempest. Then at last Mount Hermon became visible, towering over the other mountains, shining white in all the glory of new fallen snow.

Morning after morning as I sat under the pine tree and listened to the Lord and spread out before him all the questions and problems that had been lying in abeyance during the past strained, abnormal year, I found to my amazement that I was undergoing a complete mental revolution. By the end of that holiday I felt almost like a person who had been born again. A complete new attitude of mind had been created in me, and everything I looked at and listened to seemed transformed and colored by this new outlook. It was a completely new attitude towards the people of Israel. I discovered that God had been answering the prayer I had prayed so desperately when the mandate ended, and I believed he was calling me to remain in the Jewish area of

Jerusalem. I had begged him then that I might really come to love the Jewish people in a new way if I remained among them. In Haifa I discovered this had come to pass.

11 *The State of Israel*

$\mathscr{S}$urely 1948 has been one of the most momentous years in the history of the world, perhaps the most momentous since that amazing time when God himself appeared upon the earth in the form of a man and was born in Palestine as a Jew; when he walked about this country and in the great, overwhelming act of revealing himself truly, allowing the men he had made to nail him to a cross. In those days were fulfilled the things spoken long before by the mouths of the prophets, who had foretold the coming of the long-awaited Messiah and Savior.

Now nineteen centuries later, in this amazing year of 1948, another God-planned and prophet-foretold wonder has taken place—the rebirth of the unchanging, undying, unassimilated Jewish nation.

The nation that rejected their Messiah at his first coming has wandered—scattered, exiled, and persecuted—through the world ever since. On May 15 as the new state of Israel was proclaimed and the British Mandate ended. As Israel again became a nation in the land of Israel, the thirty-seventh chapter of Ezekiel was read in Hebrew over the radio—the glorious prophecy of the scattered, dry bones that were suddenly joined together with flesh and sinews and then received the life of God.

We who remained in the country while the astonishing miracle happened will never forget with what a noise and shaking those bones came together and were formed into one body and nation. It was an astonishing and awe-inspiring event. It came as the climax to thirty years of Jewish immigration to Palestine, since the Balfour Declaration in 1917, when the door of Palestine was opened at long last, and the scattered units of the Jewish nation began to return to their ancient homeland. For thirty years Jeremiah 16:16 had been happening before our eyes. Fished by Zionist propaganda and hunted by Nazi persecution, the dispersed Jewish people in every country of the world have been returning, first in small numbers, then by hundreds of thousands, to their old homeland. And on May 15, 1948, with the termination of a Gentile mandatory government, this amazing *return* culminated in the formation of the first Jewish state in the land of Israel. The bones came together, and the sinews and the flesh began to form upon them.

The noise and the shaking of war that accompanied this miracle were so great and distracting that for a time we Gentile Christians who were privileged to remain in the country scarcely realized what was happening. Life was very much a day-to-day affair, each day with its own problems and tests and trials, and an almost hour-by-hour gratitude at being

allowed to remain alive. But since the dying down of actual
warfare and the chance to take stock of the new situation,
and above all, to ponder over the Scriptures and to await
upon God in humble earnestness for understanding, the stupendous significance of the year's happenings is almost
overwhelming. God's clock has again struck an hour of
supreme importance: the restoration of Israel as a nation to
their ancient homeland, to be followed by the return of the
Messiah. How can one express the awe of such a thought?

It is true that life under the new state goes on wonderfully
much as usual. The ravages of war and the many inconveniences attached to the very unsatisfactory truces have been
minimized surprisingly quickly. We have now an Israeli
government, a new army, and a new principal language
(Hebrew). We have new currency, new stamps, new judges,
new officials, new taxes, and if one may suggest such a thing
in democratic Israel, a new aristocracy. Among so many
new and wonderful developments, we dare to hope and
believe that there will perhaps be a new tolerance and consideration meted out to the tiny Hebrew Christian community, that those Jews who believe in Christ will be allowed
to take their share in building up the new Israel, without
being penalized for their religious convictions.

I must confess, humbly and honestly, that the successful
establishment of the Jewish state in Israel came as a completely unexpected, and at first, incomprehensible surprise.
Perhaps to other Christians, especially in Palestine, the
same problem has presented itself. Many of us who believed
in the Bible prophecies concerning the final restoration of
Israel to the Promised Land and the ultimate fulfillment of
all God's purposes of blessing for them, and through them,
to the whole world, found it almost impossible to believe
that modern Zionism, which is a political and largely nonre-

ligious power, could achieve possession of the land of Israel by its own strength. If they forfeited the land through unbelief and rejection of the Messiah, how could it be possible for them to get possession of it again while still in unbelief, and with no acknowledgment, as a nation, of their dependence upon God's help and support? The whole problem may perhaps be summed up in the words of an earnest Arab Christian. He was asked if he did not believe that the Scriptures foretold the restoration of the land of Israel to the Jewish people, and he replied, "Certainly, I believe that, and expect it, but not to such an Israel as this—unbelieving, materialistic and God-rejecting."

Many of us therefore doubted very strongly whether present-day Zionism would be allowed to achieve victory and to establish the State of Israel. It seemed to us that failure and defeat were inevitable without open acknowledgment of Israel's utter dependence upon God and willingness to submit to him.

This strong conviction on my part made the very idea of remaining in Jewish Jerusalem throughout the war a nightmare to contemplate. I did not see how the Jews could hold out and thought that their defeat was only to be expected. That things turned out so differently was amazing and an utter surprise and meant a complete readjustment of thought. During those quiet weeks in Haifa I waited humbly and expectantly on God and begged to be given an understanding heart and to be shown the answer to three problems that had so perplexed me:

1. Israel is still in unbelief. Does it not contradict all God's teaching in their history if he allows them to get possession of the land by their own efforts and not by faith and obedience?

2. Israel has no right to the Promised Land while still rejecting the Messiah, for they forfeited and lost the land when they persisted in rejecting him. Surely no earthly power or government can give back what God took away?

3. How can it be fair to the Arab people already in the land? What right has Israel to come and turn them out? What right have other nations to encourage this political injustice?

Problem 1: Israel is still in unbelief.

As a nation, it is materialistic and not God-fearing. Does it not contradict all that God has taught them — that his help and presence and power among them depend upon faith and obedience — if he allows them to achieve success by their own efforts alone?

First and foremost, we must remember that the return of Israel as a nation to the Promised Land is foretold in the prophecies. It is one of the great parts of prophecy that up till now has not been fulfilled. There are passages of Scripture that suggest that Israel will be brought back to their land by the overruling of God's providence and his manipulation of circumstances, while they are still in unbelief. It is when they are in the land that the promise is to be fulfilled: "*Then* will I sprinkle clean water upon you, and ye shall be clean. . . . A new heart will I give you and a new spirit will I put within you." See, for instance, Ezekiel 36:22–38.

Second, there do not seem to be any prophecies that say definitely that the third restoration to the land will depend primarily upon faith and obedience, as were the first two deliverances from Egypt and Babylon, but it will be in the nature of a sign to the world, a tremendous challenge and warning from God. "I will sanctify my great name, which was profaned among the heathen, which ye have profaned in the midst of them, and the heathen shall know that I am the LORD, saith the Lord GOD, when I shall be sanctified in you before their eyes. For I will take you from among the heathen, and gather you out of all countries, and will bring you into your own land" (Ezek. 36:23–24).

In a very striking way God's dealings with Israel in these days is a stone of stumbling and rock of offense to the nations of the world, just as the first advent of Christ was a stone of stumbling and rock of offense to the nation of Israel. Now it is the revived nation of Israel that is parting the nations upon the right hand and the left, those who consciously or unconsciously cooperate with God's purpose for Israel's restoration and those who oppose it.

Third, we Christians must always bear in mind with repentance and humility that the Jewish people have not seen true Christianity manifestly set forth before them. Their rejection of the truth concerning the Messiah and Savior of the world is at least as much to be blamed upon the visible Christian churches as upon the Jewish people themselves. They have lived in countries where worldly, wealth-seeking, nominal Christianity has been an appalling stumbling block to their reception of the truth. The worst persecutions they have undergone have taken place in so-called Christian nations. Many and many a Jewish child has seen torture and death meted out to parents and loved ones in Russia or Poland, while a priest held aloft a cross and invoked the blessing of the Father, Son, and Holy Ghost on these outrages perpetrated in Christ's name, while the last and most ghastly persecution of all was carried out in a nominal Christian country under the Nazi regime.

It is, of course, true that God has not left himself without faithful witnesses, and that many churches and groups as well as unnumbered individuals have faithfully presented the truth and the grace of the Lord Jesus and have shown in their own lives and actions a picture of his love. But it is not to be wondered at that, surrounded as the Jewish people have been in every country by false presentations of Christianity and oppressed by scorn and persecution, they have persisted in rejecting the Christian Messiah.

It must also be remembered that in Palestine itself a whole generation of Jewish children have grown up in the settlements in total ignorance of the New Testament. They have had no Christians around them of any description. Often their ignorance of the Old Testament has been almost as complete, though this is now being remedied, and the Old Testament is being taught in the schools.

The great point, however, is that Israel is still in unbelief because the nominal churches have completely failed to challenge her with a true presentation of the Christian gospel, lived out in word and deed. And what the churches have so lamentably failed to do, God himself has undertaken at this momentous crisis. This miracle that he has wrought is his call and challenge to Israel to turn again in faith and repentance to the God of Israel and to serve him with obedience and joy. He has saved them with an outstretched arm and done for them what no human power could have done: He has brought them back from the ends of the earth, whether they wanted to come or not, and planted them again in their own land.

Fourth, he would say to Israel about this epoch-making event and sign: "I do not this for your sakes, O house of Israel, but for mine holy name's sake, which ye have profaned among the heathen, whither ye went" (Ezek. 36:22). It has been the hand of God and his outstretched arm that has accomplished this wonderful happening, not Israel's own strength and might, bravely and heroically though her people have fought and suffered. One of the most amazing characteristics of the war that has raged since the end of the mandate has been the disunity between the Arab invading armies and the different Arab governments, the apparent impossibility of their cooperating together, the internal strifes and jealousies, and above all the extraordinary fear and dread that fell upon the Arab population of Palestine, causing them to flee by the hundreds of thousands. Panic not only fell upon the civilian population, but sometimes on the invading armies too. It has seemed as though God has done again what he did in olden times when he said, "There shall no man be able to stand before you: for the LORD your God shall lay the fear of you and the dread of you upon all the land" (Deut. 11:25).

Finally, there is a very solemn warning to Israel herself in these same prophecies. It seems that full and complete victory and possession *does* depend upon whether the new Jewish state will turn to the God of Israel, openly acknowledging him and ascribing to him all the honor and victory. The state, if it would prosper and remain free, must be founded not only upon his righteous laws, but also upon personal and individual surrender to him.

If such is not the outcome of this wonderful but *partial* victory, if Israel remains in unbelief and takes credit to herself for the victories achieved, it seems certain that judgment in the form of defeat lies ahead, and disaster will overtake her here in the land of promise itself. For the "time of Jacob's trouble" cannot come to an end until Jacob becomes Israel in very truth, by worshiping and obeying Israel's God and acknowledging their Messiah and Savior. (See Jer. 30:7–9.)

Problem 2: Israel has no right in the land of Israel while still rejecting Israel's Messiah.

One cannot help feeling that this is a true objection. They have no spiritual right to the land at this stage, and here again we see the wonderful wisdom of God. For he is restoring the people of Israel to the land but is not yet restoring the land to them wholly and completely. Partition can never be called full possession, and full possession, the Scriptures seem to show clearly, will depend upon their own attitude and actions in the land. God is now affording Israel a wonderful opportunity to experience his power and might, to enjoy in a measure success and victory, and to choose, while free from persecution and exile, whether they will in very truth become *his* people or not. What the Christian church has largely failed to manifest to them of the power and grace and patience and unchanging love of God, he himself is prepared to reveal to them in the land. The very fact that he has permitted them to return while still in unbelief is another wonderful instance of his exceeding mercy and grace.

Here surely lies the stupendous privilege of the Christian church. We have a unique opportunity now to cooperate with God, in ceaseless intercession for Israel, that the miracles of spiritual rebirth may take place. We have seen the literal fulfillment of the first verses of Ezekiel 36: the birth of the new state, the forming of Israel once again into a nation. Now let the church of Christ, aflame with love for Israel, pray with one heart and mind for the coming of the life of God into the new nation and for true spiritual revival in Israel. Pray that the church in this country may be cleansed and empowered for witness as never before. Her last great work and opportunity before her Lord's return may well be to intercede for Israel and to witness a good confession, that

she may help to prepare the Jewish nation for the second
advent of their Messiah.

*Problem 3: How can it be fair to the Arab and other peoples in Pal-
estine to have their land taken from them?*

Here, indeed, is a difficult and thorny subject that we
must try and think about without prejudice. First and foremost, we need to remember that for many years the Jews
settled peacefully in the country, paying generously for
what land they occupied and settled in, settling not by right
of force or conquest, but by generous compensation. They
bought what land they occupied from the Arabs, who will-
ingly sold it for what was at the time a fair price. Land was
bought from the wealthy landowners, a number of whom
lived elsewhere and cared little for Palestine. It is true that
in this way the Arab peasants lost certain rights of grazing
and the chances of earning their living in the way they had
been accustomed to for generations. But the British were
able to offer them employment. Soon Arabs were able to
earn more in Palestine than in any of the surrounding Arab
countries, while the Zionist development of the land, as well
as the mandatory projects and improvements, undoubtedly
brought hitherto unknown prosperity to all who were willing to cooperate and to work. A great deal of the areas the
Jews now own consisted of barren, rocky, sandy, or apparently unfertile land that the Arabs themselves had never
attempted to cultivate. At the cost of immense expense,
labor, and sacrifice, the Jewish people have developed these
barren areas and made them fruitful and productive. To try
to deny them the right to govern these areas would indeed
be a political injustice. Having voluntarily received just
compensation for the lands, the Arab peoples now seem

disposed to claim the lands they sold, which are now a thousandfold increased in value.

The objection and fear felt by so many Palestinian Arabs that with immensely increased Jewish immigration into the country there would soon be a Jewish majority, and the whole land would thus come under their domination, was met by the Jewish people with the very fair offer to accede to the proposal to partition the land, and that they would thus have full rights to administer and govern their own paid-for areas only.

It must be admitted, as a great misfortune, that the Jewish people permitted the dissident terrorist groups to have such a powerful influence and to commit so many acts of violence that the Palestinian Arabs too often had cause for alarm and dread, and the Jewish cause was terribly prejudiced in the eyes of the world. On these dissident groups must rest the bulk of the blame for the increasing hatred and fear of Zionism felt by other peoples in the land. That many of them were true patriots and sincerely convinced that these deeds of violence were for the ultimate good of their people only makes it the more tragic and lamentable.

Then, too, Zionist propaganda has not always been wise or helpful. Statements have been made and claims advanced by certain sections that were calculated to foment fear, resentment, and suspicion among the Arab peoples. It is a matter for great thankfulness that the recent first general election in Israel has revealed that the vast majority of Israeli citizens are solidly behind the wiser and more moderate parties, and that only a very small percentage of the population are in favor of the extremist groups.

The blame for the tragic and appalling problem of the Arab refugees is not to be laid wholly on the Jews. The overboastful propaganda of the Arabs made its contribution to this problem, as well as the claims advanced by certain Jewish extremists. While the terrorists on both sides have, by their deeds of violence, added to the suspicion, hatred, and fear that have resulted in the Arab peasants fleeing in their thousands to Transjordan and elsewhere.

In conclusion, one other thing remains to be said. It is not easy to say, and harder still not to appear to condemn and criticize at a time when the Christians of Palestine are undergoing such bitter trial and testing, but perhaps we have needed such a time as this to make us willing to face up to the truth about ourselves. If the establishment of a Jewish state in the land of Israel, after an exile of nearly two thousand years, is a significant challenge from God to the whole world, it is perhaps in a special way, a sign and warning to the Christian churches in the Middle East. They have been involved in terrible loss, hardship, and calamity, and we cannot help but feel that God himself has been speaking to us, perhaps judging and testing our witness and our profession of faith. He has brought into fiery trial not only the ancient eastern churches, but the Roman and Protestant churches too. We have been tried and found wanting. This scattering of the Christian communities and the exile of so many Christians in other countries is perhaps a solemn and merciful warning from God that we had a name to live and yet were dead.

No one who has lived in this country, and perhaps scarcely any thoughtful person who has visited it as a tourist or a pilgrim, can fail to be painfully aware of so much worldliness, materialism, commercialism, and formalism in the churches in the Holy Land. We were nearly bankrupt spiritually. Our sacred places were too often like the temple in the days when our Lord was here, places where the sightseer was asked for gifts rather than where the pilgrim was invited to pray. We were in some measure as guilty as the Jews of our Lord's own time when he said, "This House shall be called a house of prayer, but ye have made it a den of thieves."

May it not be that God has permitted this fiery trial to come upon the churches in Palestine for a double purpose of grace and blessing. First, that we may be brought to realize our spiritual bankruptcy and the emptiness and formalism of much that we looked upon as religious faith, so that stripped of our self-complacency, and with our faith tested to the very foundation, we may turn to God in penitence for cleansing and renewal.

As we pray for a spiritual rebirth for Israel, let us humbly acknowledge our own desperate need for a spiritual rebirth too. We who have been foreign missionaries and teachers must surely acknowledge our own share of blame. We may well ask ourselves humbly and honestly, "If we had been faithful to the Word of God and courageously taught the Scriptures in connection with God's purposes for Israel, need the Arab Christian communities and congregations ever have been found among the enemies of Israel?"

May it not be also that this testing and judgment that has come upon the church of Christ in the country of its birthplace is also a warning to other churches throughout the world. There are many signs that we may be nearing the end of this "age" and that the return of our Lord may be imminent. It was he who said that the generation that saw the beginning of the signs of the end would be the same generation that sees their conclusion (Matt. 24:33–34).

What sort of people then ought we to be at such a momentous hour as this? Are not these happenings a great challenge to the church to make herself ready for her Lord's coming? To her the bridegroom would say, "I counsel thee to buy of me gold tried in the fire, that thou mayest be rich; and white raiment, that thou mayest be clothed, . . . and anoint thine eyes with eyesalve, that thou mayest see. As many as I love I rebuke and chasten: be zealous therefore, and repent" (Rev. 3:18–19).

"Knowing the time, that now it is high time to awake out of sleep: for now is our salvation nearer than when we believed. The night is far spent, the day is at hand: let us therefore cast off the works of darkness, and let us put on the armour of light" (Rom. 13:11–12).

12 *Watchmen on the Walls of Jerusalem*

When the British Mandate ended on May 14, 1948, twelve foreign Protestant missionaries remained in the Jewish quarter of Jerusalem, two men and ten women. There were others, of course, in Arab Jerusalem. A handful of Hebrew Christian helpers and believers with Palestinian passports also stayed behind. We missionaries belonged to six different nations: There were two Finns, one Swede, two Dutch, two Swiss, two American, and three British, owing allegiance to at least six different sections of the Christian church.

Up to this time we had not known one another at all intimately, nor had we worked together, and some of us had not even met before. Jerusalem during the mandate had been a gathering place for missionaries on a large scale. Over sixty different Protestant societies and groups had been listed as working in Jerusalem alone, and it was estimated that there were far more missionaries to the square mile in Palestine than in any other part of the world.

It is safe to say that if the task of selecting twelve missionaries to remain behind had been left to the twelve of us who did stay, we would not, at that period, have chosen each other. A few of us were already intimate friends, but as a group we were more like strangers when thus left together in a Jerusalem besieged by Arab armies. None of us had been asked to remain, but each stayed because of a clear, personal call from God.

As so many people left the country, we often felt like Gideon's little company as we were sifted down and down until it seemed as though no one would be left at all. God himself did the sifting and the separating and the choosing. A very surprising choice it looked to us when, after the first dreadful month of siege, the first, short truce enabled us to leave our different compounds and to make some kind of move towards each other in order to find mutual support. We were more or less separated by natural barriers, differences of language, nationality, theological outlook, denominational differences, and above all, temperamental contrasts.

What a weak, rather pathetic little group we were from the world's standpoint. We had nothing very startling to display among us in the way of learning, scholarship, talents, and wisdom. Ronald was the youngest, having been in the country only a year, while the rest of us were nearly all old hands who had at least a smattering of Hebrew. We were very ordinary people indeed and very human in our temperamental differences and weaknesses. Looking back now to those early weeks, I find myself smiling and blushing, half with astonishment and half with shame, as I recollect in what light esteem I in my blindness held some of that tiny group. Lilly, of course, was a tried and proved friend; so was Aili. Mrs. Gibson, Ruth, and Ronald were obviously comrades to be deeply grateful for, and I did thank God for them daily. The others were nearly strangers to me. Yet if I were asked to write another list now I would not omit a single name.

Some things, however, we did all have in common. We loved our Lord and wanted to serve him, and believed that he had asked us to remain behind for a purpose. We all believed in his promises in connection with Israel and her final restoration to spiritual life and blessing, and we looked with joyful hope and expectation for the Lord's return. When we found ourselves left as a tiny Christian remnant in Jewish Jerusalem, with our congregations scattered to the four winds and all of our usual channels of missionary work no longer functioning, the great question facing us all was, "What is God's purpose in leaving us here? What special work has he for us to do?"

God seemed to have laid upon the hearts of some of us, in a very special way, the thought from Isaiah 62:6–7:

> *I have set watchmen upon thy walls, O Jerusalem, which shall never hold their peace day nor night: ye that make mention of the LORD, keep not silence, and give him no rest, till he establish, and till he make Jerusalem a praise in the earth.*

We have come to believe that God left us here as a little band of watchmen, with four responsibilities:

1. To watch and recognize what is happening and to act as God's reporters, so that his church may know how to pray and be challenged to intercede for Israel.
2. To intercede with God day and night, that all his purposes and plans in connection with Israel may come to pass.
3. To witness to the people of Israel round about us.
4. To claim the complete fulfilment of Ezekiel 37: That as Israel has now been born as a nation, the wind of heaven, the Holy Spirit, may breathe upon her, that she shall live in the true spiritual sense.

We know that there is a great army of intercessors all over the world, praying for Israel at this time. We who have been privileged to remain in Jerusalem in these historic days would like to report to you what is happening, that you may better understand how to pray. Like Gideon's little band, our usual missionary weapons have been swept away, and we are left with lamps and trumpets only—lamps for witness and trumpets for warning. I should like to feel that this book goes forth as a peal from one of the trumpets—a call and a challenge to God's believing people everywhere—to pray and intercede as never before for the coming to pass of God's word and of his purposes here in Israel.

Perhaps, as never before in our missionary work, we are learning the power and importance of united, believing prayer as the greatest weapon that God has given to his people.

For months past we have heard the besieging Arab armies and their heavy batteries assaulting this city of Jerusalem in which we live in a vain attempt to break through and take it. Now we have come to realize that we, the whole church of Christ, are to make an assault by prayer, faith, and witness not only upon Jerusalem, but upon the whole state of Israel. We seem to be left with one weapon only—believing, importunate prayer.

Perhaps much of our missionary work in the past has seemed ineffective because with other avenues and channels of work at our disposal we did not give this mightiest of all weapons its rightful place as our first and supreme work. We allowed prayer to be crowded out by a timetable full of other good works. Now having been stripped of nearly every other missionary weapon, and left with prayer alone, we have become convinced that this is the vital weapon he would have us use in these days. We should rediscover and use it to the utmost under his leadership to assault the powers of darkness and take possession of Jerusalem for Jesus the Messiah.

It has been this ever-deepening sense of the urgency for united prayer and intercession that has drawn our tiny little Christian remnant together. We are becoming welded into one body, praying together, worshiping together, and working together.

As soon as the situation became easier and the shelling ceased in the second truce, we began meeting together every week for united prayer, each time assembling in a different Christian home. There is nothing like united prayer for drawing Christians together and breaking down barriers, and certainly these weekly gatherings have become a blessing far beyond anything we dreamed of. God is awakening in us a great expectancy and a longing for spiritual quickening and revival, that our weak and feeble little group may receive the same enduement with power that was granted to the first small group of Christians in Jerusalem. We, too, would claim the promise that he gave, "Ye shall receive power, after that the Holy Ghost is come upon you: and ye shall be witnesses unto me both in Jerusalem, and in all

Judea, and in Samaria, and unto the uttermost part of the earth" (Acts 1:8).

We realize and confess that what we have most lacked is love. We therefore pray for the revival among ourselves of the fire of the Holy Spirit's burning love. As the fire fell upon the early church, so we pray that it may fall upon this remnant of the church and fuse us into one body filled with holy love.

This book is meant to be, if God will so bless it, a call from the watchmen in Jerusalem. May it come to you who read it as a clear challenge and appeal, a note of warning as well as of triumph and expectation. May you hear it as a call to constant prayer and intercession for the revival of Christ's church in Palestine and for the spiritual rebirth of the Jewish nation.

"Rejoice ye with Jerusalem, and be glad with her, all ye that love her: rejoice for joy with her, all ye that mourn for her. . . . For thus saith the LORD, Behold I will extend peace to her like a river, and the glory of the Gentiles like a flowing stream. . . . As one whom his mother comforteth, so will I comfort you; and ye shall be comforted in Jerusalem" (Isa. 66:10, 12, 13).

"I have set watchmen upon thy walls, O Jerusalem, which shall never hold their peace day nor night: ye that make mention of the LORD, keep not silence, and give him no rest, till he establish, and till he make Jerusalem a praise in the earth" (Isa. 62:6–7).

Epilogue:
The Situation Now

*I*srael's journey into national maturity has been tortuous. For the first nineteen years (1948–1967), Jerusalem was a divided city. Canon Hugh Jones, rector of Christ Church in the Old City, had to seek permission from both sides whenever he needed to visit his own parish church during that time!

Strange to say that the world community said little when Jordan annexed both Jerusalem and the West Bank in April 1950 but erupted with uproar when Israel declared the undivided city to be its eternal capital after the Six Day War in 1967. A number of embassies were moved to Tel Aviv as a protest at that time.

Following terrorist activities in 1972, including the hijacking of planes, letter bombs, and massacres at Lod Airport and the Munich Olympic Games, the Yom Kippur War of 1973 broke out. It almost spelled the end of Israel as a sovereign state. In more recent times, both the Intifada and the Gulf War posed ominous threats. At the present time the peace process makes only halting progress.

Yet the burgeoning of the state has been little less than a miracle. From day one, Israel has boasted an incredibly sophisticated welfare state. Against the odds, the economy has boomed, to the benefit of both Arabs and Jews. The countryside has blossomed. And the renovated city of Jerusalem is "beautiful for situation, the joy of the whole earth."

CMJ's ministry in the land has also developed since 1948. The former CMS (Church Missionary Society) clinic at Lydda was opened again by CMJ in December 1956. In the following year, Ruth Clark retired from the Jerusalem School and took charge of a new reading room in Tel Aviv, financed in the main by The Friends of Israel Gospel Ministry of America. Boys' camps, run by Rev. Ronald Adeney, became a regular feature of the Society's work at this time, while Mr. I. Ball, a Romanian Jew, ran a book depot in Israel's second city. In 1960 Dr. Billy Graham preached to a congregation of more than a thousand at St. Peter's in Tel Aviv.

For some time the society had wanted to open a center of reconciliation in the north. So when its Terjubilee Fund in 1959 realized £32,000, the former home of a wealthy Arab was bought in March 1961 at Isfiyah, east of Haifa. Today Stella Carmel is growing apace and realizing many of the hopes its pioneers longed to see.

There were violent demonstrations by Orthodox Jews against Christian schools in 1963. But after an initial setback, the school in Jerusalem slowly picked up. The hospital buildings, which continue to house the school, had been handed back to CMJ in 1953. By 1965 there were 120 pupils enrolled, fourteen of whom were Jewish and twelve of whom were Muslims. Following the Six Day War in 1967, Christ Church in Jerusalem was able to come into its own again. At that stage there were more than three hundred pupils between ages five and seventeen from more than forty nationalities being taught in the former hospital.

Much of this new advance in the work was due to Canon Jones, "a man of wise counsel, charm and never-failing sympathy." Sadly, he was forced to retire because of ill health in April 1963 and died just over a year later. He was replaced, first by Canon Roger Allison, whose original appointment to CMJ's mission in Warsaw had been frustrated by the outbreak of the Second World War; then by Canon Ronald Adeney. Since then, Rev. David Price and Canon Michael Bulman have headed up the work. The present Israel director is Rev. John Claydon.

By 1965 the clinic at Lydda was closed. However, the Book Corner at Ramleh proved a useful asset to CMJ's work over the next five years.

Meanwhile, the work at Immanuel House to the south of Tel Aviv went ahead in fits and starts. This former hotel had come into the possession of CMJ in 1927 and was originally used as the English High School of Jaffa. But it was commandeered first by the British in 1947, then by the Israelis. By the time it was handed back to CMJ in 1953, it was in a very run-down condition. Mercifully, a plan to sell the building came to nothing, for when the winds of the Spirit stirred in the early seventies, the work began to grow again. The basement, once used for interning Arab dissidents, became a children's day care. The house's library, supplemented by

H. L. Ellison's personal collection of books, formed the base for a study program, which has now been replaced by the King of Kings Bible School, serving many of the forty-five Messianic congregations in the land.

So the several centers of service that are mentioned here and there in Hannah's journal have experienced something of a resurrection since the Sincere Truce brought an end to the conflict so vividly chronicled in her book.

Back in 1958, the society's annual review had prophesied that "some day a Christian church will spring up among the Jews in Israel, and we must be ready with our contribution." Today that is a reality, as congregations of Jewish people, who cling tenaciously to their Jewishness but recognize Yeshua (Jesus) as their Messiah, come into being throughout Israel.

Today's visitor to the Holy Land can only marvel at all that has happened in the fifty years since independence. The price has been high. Men and women on both sides of the seemingly never-ending conflict bear many a scar. And there must yet be sacrifices on all sides if the people's hopes for peace are to be realized. Yet, prejudices apart, the possibilities for progress are incalculable. And God remains the Lord of history.

It is heavenly to visit Christ Church, just inside the Jaffa Gate, opposite the citadel, and to reflect on all that has happened there since Bishop Michael Solomon Alexander laid the foundation stone back in the 1840s. To one side is a fine coffee shop where Jews, Arabs, Armenians, and ex-patriates serve together. Next door is a well-appointed book shop. Within the Christ Church compound itself stand the two wings of a hostel that caters for tourists, a dining room undergoing extensions, a fascinating little museum, a small school for the children of Messianic Jews, the office of a tourist company: *Shoresh* (meaning "root"), and the church itself.

On Saturday afternoons, this former British consul's private chapel, built on the grounds of what had been Herod the Great's palace garden in second temple times, is the venue for a Hebrew-speaking Jewish congregation. While in the evening of "the first day of the week," a growing congregation of Romanians also uses the church's facilities. On Sundays, folks from all over the world gather to worship under the leadership of the present rector and his wife, Rev. Ray and Jill Lockhart.

Only a few years ago, the *Jerusalem Post* aptly described Christ Church as "The church which loves the Jews." But it has a heart for neighboring Arabs and Armenians as well, for the gospel of God's reconciling love, which is "to the Jew first," is for the Gentile too (Rom. 1:16).

The newly refurbished school in the Street of the Prophets, northwest of the Old City, has more than three hundred pupils and some Jewish teachers who serve alongside staff drawn from other countries. The Society's long-standing presence in the land gives it a unique status as a body that inherits legal immunities granted under the mandate and enshrined in Israeli law. Long may its work, destined to become even more indigenous than at the present time, continue to honor that privilege in a way that blesses people of all nationalities who live in Jerusalem, "the city of the great King" (Ps. 48:2; Matt. 5:35).

—John Wood

Table
of Dates

*(Connected with the establish-
ment of the state of Israel)*

1897	Birth of Zionism. First Zionist Congress.
1914–1918	First World War.
1917	The Balfour Declaration, permitting the formation of a Jewish National Home in Palestine.
1918–1948	British Mandate over Palestine.
1920	First Arab anti-Jewish disturbances.
1929	Arab anti-Jewish outbreak in Palestine (chiefly in the Hebron area).
1933–1945	Nazi persecution of the Jews in Europe.
1936–1939	Widespread Arab anti-Jewish disturbances.
1939	White Paper forbidding further sale of land to the Jews and drastically restricting Jewish immigration.

1939–1948	Illegal immigration.
1939–1945	Second World War.
1945–1948	Cyprus internment camps for illegal immigrants to Palestine.
1945–1948	Jewish antigovernment disturbances, led by dissident terrorist groups, as a reaction to the White Paper restrictions.
1946	*July 22.* Blowing up of Government Secretarial Offices in the King David Hotel, with loss of one hundred lives.
1947	Kidnapping of British officials by Jewish terrorists and hanging of two British sergeants. "Operation Polly." Evacuation from Palestine of British women and children.
1947	*November 29.* United Nations voted for the partition of Palestine.
	December 2. Arab strike and outbreak of war.
1948	*January–May.* Battle of the Roads.
	May 14. End of the British Mandate.
	May 15. Proclamation of the new state of Israel. Invasion of Palestine by Arab armies.
	May 15–June 11. Complete siege of Jerusalem.
	June 11–July 9. The first cease-fire.
	July 9–18. Resumption of hostilities.
	July 18. The second truce.
	August–December. Unsatisfactory truce and many outbreaks of fighting.
	September 17. Assassination of Count Bernadotte, the mediator, by Jewish terrorists.

November–December. Fighting in the south of
 Palestine against the Egyptians.
December 3. Jerusalem's "Sincere Truce."
 Complete cessation of hostilities for the
 first time since November 27, 1947.

1949 *January 25*. First general elections in the state
 of Israel.
January 29. Great Britain recognized Israel.

Notes

1. The partition of Jerusalem remained until reunification after the Six Day War (June 5–10, 1967).

2. Lilly Wreschner, who had helped in Hannah's village work, later served in the north of Israel, before retiring to her native Switzerland.

3. "Laurie" was of course Ruth Laurence, who had been Hannah's closest associate in the work of reaching Jewish settlements and Arab villages from 1937 on.

4. The other two members of the mission were: Rev. (later Canon) Hugh Jones, rector of Christ Church; and Miss E. E. Abramson, who was in charge of the junior school based on the compound.

5. Miss Aili Havas from Finland had helped Hannah learn Hebrew and had assisted Hannah in her village work.

6. While taking a brief break back in Britain, Rev. Hugh Jones of Christ Church wrote his own review of events in Jerusalem, which was published in the October edition of CMJ's monthly magazine. The article bore witness to the nearness of God's presence and the power of prayer in their lives. It also reflected on the achievements

of Israel's fledgling forces in driving the Arab invaders back. At the same time it rued the activities of extremists on both sides of the conflict who caused so much prejudice and frustrated hopes of agreement. By their love for both Jews and Arabs in the divided city, CMJ staff members were able to pay Arab employees on behalf of their Jewish employers, and vice versa. Hugh Jones expressed the hope that by making the Society's hospital available to the Jewish authorities free of charge, the cause of Christ would be promoted. As it was, more than one thousand sick and wounded were treated there during one fortnight in June. Miss Clark was doing a magnificent work in the school. But she could not go on doing this single-handedly for much longer. Meanwhile, it was becoming clear that discrimination against Hebrew Christians in the city was prompted more by political than by religious motives. The article finished by lamenting the desecration of Jewish holy places in the Old City and requesting prayer for the many unfortunate Arabs who had fled their homes "in fear and terror."

...Other great titles from
Broadman & Holman

In The Lion's Den
Nina Shea

More Christians have died for their faith in the 20th century than in the previous nineteen centuries combined. This book documents the persecution of Christians in China, Pakistan, Saudi Arabia, and other countries, examining the reasons why American churches have remained silent on such a critical issue. A special section offers specific suggestions for action to raise the awareness level of religious persecution, and encourage authorities around the world to let Christians worship and teach in peace.

0-8054-6357-7

The Christian Traveler's Guide To The Holy Land
Charles H. Dyer & Gregory A. Hatteberg

More Christians are traveling to the Holy Land each year (an estimated 800,000 in 1996) to experience its history and mystery first-hand. This practical travel guide is designed to help visitors recognize and appreciate what they see there in a Christian context. This informative manual explains how best to prepare physically and spiritually for a trip to the Holy Land. It provides biblical and historical insights to make your trip go smoothly. Also, includes sites in Aegean, Athens, Corinth, Crete, Ephesus, and Jordan.

0-8054-0156-3

The Power Of Prayer And Fasting
Ronnie Floyd

Although prayer has always been an integral part of our relationship with God, fasting has largely been ignored by Christians. Now there is a rising groundswell of interest in utilizing both prayer and fasting as a Scripture-based means for growing closer to God. *The Power Of Prayer And Fasting* includes a practical guide for those readers interested in experiencing a one-day, three-day, seven-day, or forty-day spiritual fast.

0-8054-0164-4

Experiencing God - Now Available in Paperback!
Henry T. Blackaby & Claude V. King

God reveals himself to each of us in special and exceptional ways, so our perception of him is unique. This remarkable book will help any believer renew and revitalize his love for the Lord by seeing His love for us. *Experiencing God* is designed to help each of us recognize our own personal relationship with God as He reveals His divine plan and guiding hand. Even as we try to understand Him, God comes alongside us to accomplish His work through us.

0-8054-0197-0

Also available:
Experiencing God (hardcover, revised)	0-8054-0196-2
Experiencing God (audio version)	0-8054-1150-X
Experiencing God Day-By-Day Devotional/Journal	0-8054-6298-8

Available at fine Christian bookstores everywhere